Redefining U.S. Education

A Systematic Approach to Teaching

Redefining U.S. Education

A Systematic Approach to Teaching

William F. Roth and Ian M. Roth

CRC Press
Taylor & Francis Group
Boca Raton   London   New York

CRC Press is an imprint of the
Taylor & Francis Group, an **informa** business

A PRODUCTIVITY PRESS BOOK

CRC Press
Taylor & Francis Group
6000 Broken Sound Parkway NW, Suite 300
Boca Raton, FL 33487-2742

© 2016 by Taylor & Francis Group, LLC
CRC Press is an imprint of Taylor & Francis Group, an Informa business

No claim to original U.S. Government works

Printed on acid-free paper
Version Date: 20150526

International Standard Book Number-13: 978-1-4987-3355-7 (Hardback)

Library of Congress Cataloging-in-Publication Data

Roth, William F.
    Redefining U.S. education : a systematic approach to teaching / William F. Roth and Ian M. Roth.
        pages cm
    Includes bibliographical references and index.
    ISBN 978-1-4987-3355-7 (alk. paper)
    1. Education--United States--History. I. Roth, Ian M. II. Title.

LA205.R66 2015
370.973--dc23   2015005097

Visit the Taylor & Francis Web site at
http://www.taylorandfrancis.com

and the CRC Press Web site at
http://www.crcpress.com

Printed and bound in Great Britain by
TJ International Ltd, Padstow, Cornwall

This book is dedicated to Kristine Mednansky, our editor at Productivity Press, with thanks for her hard work and continual encouragement, and especially because she is unafraid to look over the edge.

Contents

Preface

Redefining U.S. Education: A Systematic Approach to Teaching
presents a new model for primary- and secondary-level education that solves two-centuries-old dilemmas through the more
effective use of technology. The book begins by discussing
the role education should play in the modern world. It then
explores the philosophical and theoretical roots of the U.S.
education system developed in Europe several centuries ago,
introducing the first major dilemma addressed even then—
should emphasis be on ensuring that all students reach a
defined level of expertise or on encouraging individual students to develop their potential to the fullest possible extent?
The book then traces the history of education theory in the
United States from early colonial days to the present, introducing a second major challenge still being struggled with—what
degree of curriculum standardization should we strive for in
order to "level the playing field?"

Next, the book returns to Europe and the Bologna Process,
identifying its advantages and shortcomings as an attempt at
standardization. It then travels to Japan, a country that represents probably the epitome in terms of standardization, and
discusses the damage this over-emphasis has done to Japanese
society, and especially to the Japanese education system.

Finally, the book returns to the United States and presents
a new paradigm for primary and secondary education that
deals with the initial dilemma introduced—group versus
the individual—as well as with the standardization issue by

utilizing technology in a more effective manner. The paradigm does so by allowing students to use computer programs to progress at their own rate in subjects they enjoy and excel at while, concurrently, ensuring that they get the basics—both academic and social. This new paradigm forces changes in our grade-level structure, in the way classes are run, and in the way subjects are taught and students are graded.

Authors

William F. Roth, **MSW**, **PhD**, is currently a professor at Kutztown University in Pennsylvania, where he teaches courses in strategic planning, organization design, ethics, and management theory. Previously, he taught for 16 years at DeSales University, where he held the McCabe Endowed Chair for Business and Society. Dr. Roth earned his PhD at The Wharton School, his master's in social work at the University of Pennsylvania, and his bachelor's in economic geography at Dartmouth College. As a consultant, Dr. Roth has worked on design and regional planning projects in Saudi Arabia, Iran, Mexico, and several locations in the United States. Previously, he spent 5 years with the poverty program and the civil rights movement in the Deep South. In addition to this book, Dr. Roth has authored eight others, the last two, *Comprehensive Healthcare for the U.S.: An Idealized Model* and *Out of the Box Thinking for Successful Managers*, published by Productivity Press. Sixty of his articles have been featured in a wide range of professional journals. Dr. Roth also writes fiction and has published several prize winning short stories.

Ian M. Roth, **MS**, graduated from Vassar College with his BA in philosophy. He then earned his MS in global and international education from Drexel University, where his thesis addressed using learning technology to teach multiculturalism in Japanese primary schools. Ian has been living in Japan since college and has taught there at the primary, secondary, and university levels. Currently, he is studying for his PhD in organizational systems at Saybrook University in San Francisco.

Chapter 1

Growth versus Development

1.1 A More Balanced Perspective?

Our societal ethic is in transition. We are shifting gradually from the *growth ethic* to the *development ethic*. The growth ethic, which drove the Industrial Revolution, basically says that only those things that can be measured quantitatively should be taken into consideration when attempting to improve our quality of life. It is a product of the U.S.'s love affair with the *scientific method* that has been the wellspring of our tremendous economic and technological advancements. "Growth," by definition, is based on the ongoing desire to get bigger. This ongoing quest to gain "more" of things that are physically measurable and frequently limited creates a competitive environment.

The oncoming development ethic, which incorporates the growth ethic into something much richer, is actually a product of ancient Greek philosophy. Aristotle is, perhaps, its main architect. He said that life has "three primary dimensions— *making, doing, and knowing.*" "Making" has to do with the production of things, including the material goods necessary for survival as well as those desired. "Doing" involves the quest for moral virtue, with *happiness* being the essence of this virtue. Aristotle said that the quest for happiness was basically a selfish one, but that man should realize cannot achieve personal happiness without taking into account the happiness of others. "Knowing," the third primary dimension, concerns to gaining the knowledge necessary to succeed at "making" and "doing."

Aristotle believed that our major objective should not be to simply "grow" in terms of the numbers, but to realize and enjoy our positive human potential to the fullest possible extent. To do so, Aristotle and other advocates of the development ethic believed that four societal inputs are necessary. The first is adequate wealth (*plenty*) produced by a healthy economy. The second is a system of governance (*good*) on all levels (national, local, and workplace) that facilitates development and protects against those who would block it. The third is access to the necessary educational vehicle (*truth*) that provides the opportunity to learn how to learn. The fourth is an environment that encourages development by both stimulating and soothing (*beauty*).

All these four inputs are required for us to develop our potential fully, but the most important one, the one upon which the others depend, is "plenty." Historically, cultures that have made the greatest contributions have all been built on a strong economic foundation. Without a solid foundation of "plenty," a foundation that generates sufficient wealth, the other required inputs are more difficult, if not impossible, to achieve. (Roth, 2005, p. 53)

The development ethic believes that gaining control over these resources and over our lives in general is critical. It says that while scientific method remains important to our advancement, incorporating human values into the equation is equally as important. The development ethic encourages cooperation as the most effective means of achieving the necessary balance. It says that once we have realized our potential we should turn around and use that potential to help improve society and generate more of the inputs necessary to facilitate the developmental efforts of others.

It is interesting to note that in the early history of the United States, some of our most noted leaders were concerned with introducing the development ethic to society. Thomas Jefferson, John Adams, and Benjamin Franklin spent several years in the drawing rooms of Paris as part of a delegation sent to convince the French to aid the newly formed country in its struggle to gain independence from Great Britain. There they took part in conversations flavored by renewed interest in ancient Greek philosophy and became familiar with the concept.

1.2 Evolution of Society's Shaping Ethic

Actually, the development ethic has popped up periodically throughout the course of western history. It was a cornerstone to the ancient Greece civilization. The Romans, who followed Greece as the major power in that part of the world, adopted it and built upon it one of the most progressive and long-lasting empires in history.

After that, however, things went downhill rapidly. Europe, beset by invasion, famine, rampant disease, continual conflict, and ignorance, entered the Dark Ages. The nobility's main interest during this period was in learning how to wage better wars. The only educated class was the priesthood, which used this advantage to dominate the political scene.

The Dark Ages led into the Medieval Period that began roughly (very roughly) about 500 AD. During the Medieval Period the quality of life improved a bit, but not very much. The life expectancy for those who survived infancy hovered around the 30s, and, as a result, the driving force in society became the *survival ethic*.

During the ensuing Renaissance Period (roughly about 1300–1500), as a result of increased contact and trade with other parts of the world, life did improve tremendously, at least for the upper class. The development ethic was revived, with emphasis shifting to leading a balanced life. The *Renaissance Man* was good at business (plenty), a wise and compassionate leader (good), well educated (truth), and a practitioner of the arts—music, painting, etc. (beauty). By the end of the Renaissance, the middle class had become the driving force behind economic growth. Merchants realized that the most important input for development was wealth and spent their lives accumulating it, mainly through trade.

Emphasis during the Protestant Reformation Period (roughly around 1500–1650) that followed the Renaissance Period was on increasing the amount of general wealth available. The belief was that hard work led to increased wealth which, in turn, led to better opportunities for overall development. This translated to the *work ethic*, which is still popular today as a guiding force for many.

Due to the increasing amounts of wealth generated during the Protestant Reformation Period and owing to the greater distribution of that wealth amongst a greater portion of the population, Europe next entered the Enlightenment Period (roughly about 1650–1800) believing that everybody could now participate in the development of their potential. Aristotle's teachings came into vogue again. Leading thinkers during the Enlightenment Period began designing the social systems—the economic systems, the educational systems, the governmental systems, the city planning systems—which were important to the development of that potential.

However, it was eventually realized that even though society now had the social system designs necessary for universal development, it continued to lack in the necessary wealth needed to put them into place. So, during the early Industrial Revolution, first Europe, and then the United States went back to generating the necessary wealth. Emphasis was now on growth as defined by the amount of wealth available, the number of automobiles and homes and widgets and pumpkins and pairs of shoes possessed. The *growth ethic* replaced the development ethic and has prevailed into modern times. More was better; the numbers were what society paid attention to.

Obviously, in today's world, we have generated enough wealth to return to the development ethic as our driving force, at least in western society. But in the United States, at least, we are having a hard time getting there, and we are having a hard time turning the corner. The growth ethic is much easier to deal with. Its rewards are more obvious and short term, while its failures, in most cases, tend to be intangible, evident only in the long term and easily ignored.

1.3 Academia Is Slow to Catch on

The academic community should be one of the leaders in the movement to adopt the development ethic in the United States. But the academic community is having trouble accepting it. The modifications necessary—due to a variety of factors ranging from tenure, to rampant territorialism, to rigid hierarchies, to an overpowering bureaucracy, to the mold mentality, to the ivory tower mentality, to an unwillingness to take full advantage of technology—are not occurring as rapidly as desired. The academic community, for the most part, continues to base its approach on a growth ethic mentality.

For example, education is still fragmented, still based on the analytical, break-it-down-and-learn-the-parts model that is foundational to scientific method and to growth ethic thinking. Classes for English, math, social studies, science, and art are still taught separately. This might be considered by some to be a necessity during the early stages of the education process in order to teach primary skills, but the mindset persists all the way into the graduate level. MBA programs, for example, teach finance, planning, human resources, marketing, ethics, and production separately, without the necessary attempts at integration, despite the fact that integration is critical for the full development of potential.

For example, teachers in the traditional growth-oriented classroom setting focused on developing a pedagogy that facilitates standardization and also facilitates all students reaching that level of learning where they are economically productive, where they can help generate wealth, and where they can help generate more of everything. In the workplace, standardization, until very recently, has been the key to increased productivity—the standardization of both technology and processes. This focus has spilled over into academia.

The problem with such spill over is that people are different from machines and processes, a fact that has been largely ignored. As a result, our education system, due to circumstances beyond its control, has become a great equalizer. Rather than a system that encourages students to focus on their individual strengths, they frequently struggle to do so, and one has to struggle for so long before he or she simply shrugs, shuts down, and falls into line.

A growing number of educators are beginning to believe that as we move into a different kind of world with different possibilities, this traditional approach to teaching is no longer the most productive, rather, in fact, it is becoming increasingly counter-productive. A growing number of educators are also beginning to understand that if we are to continue progressing as a nation, we need to move onto the development ethic, where more emphasis must be placed on the development of each student's unique potential.

Is this possible? Yes, it is. For one thing, the necessary technology has finally arrived. Computers are going to make the difference. They are going to allow us to finally enter the "new world" in the realm of education. But before getting into what is going on today and suggesting changes, we need to understand the evolution of the US public education system. We need to talk about how we got to where we are in terms of our system's strengths and weaknesses. To facilitate this effort, we will draw from the experiences of two other major societies, also known for their progressiveness: the societies of Europe and Japan. We shall try to learn from their successes and failures by relating those successes and failures to our own situation.

As a first step in this process, we will discuss the evolution of education in Europe where the U.S. system finds its roots, where most of the philosophy upon which our system is or, at least, was originally based evolved over a period of more than 1000 years, contributed by some of the western world's greatest minds.

Chapter 2

The Historic Evolution of Education in Europe: A Brief Synopsis

2.1 Only for the Chosen

During the previously mentioned Medieval Period in Europe that began as part of the Dark Ages following the collapse of the Roman Empire, education was controlled by the Church. Most schools were affiliated with cathedrals, and their curriculum was dictated by the Catholic hierarchy. The main purpose of these schools was to train clergy. The only subjects, besides religion, being taught were reading, writing, and sometimes Latin. Eventually, owing to the influence of humanists, the curriculum expanded to include the study of Greek and Roman writings.

There were two reasons for this elitist attitude. One was the Church's belief that education could be dangerous; that it encouraged questioning and might lead parishioners into sinful thought, into questioning the Church's dictates and control. For their own good, therefore, it was best to keep the common folk illiterate in order to keep them from gaining access to the information and knowledge that led to such questioning. The second less-philosophical reason arose from the fact that each document and each book produced had to be hand-written with a quill pen and a pot of ink. The eraser had not yet been invented, so any mistake made, any blotch, or any misshapen letter necessitated rewriting the entire page. Finishing a complete document sometimes took months or even years. Obviously, at that rate of production, relatively few books existed. Those that did exist were treasured and carefully guarded. Passing them around didn't make much sense in terms of wear and tear; so they were kept locked safely away in somebody's library, inaccessible to the masses.

The opportunity to gain education improved somewhat during the Renaissance. However, it was during the Protestant Reformation that it really took off. This happened, again, for two reasons. One again had to do with values. The Protestant Reformation resulted at least as much from economic as it did from religious considerations. Because of new markets, new advances in science and technology, and new sources of raw materials, including the North and South American continents, greater amounts of wealth could be generated, and everybody wanted a share of it.

The new Protestant religion gave commoners the rationalization they needed to break away from the paternalism of the Catholic Church and to try their luck. It did so by reshaping a traditional Catholic concept, that of "good works." The concept of good works had to do with efforts contributed by parishioners to the community, say, to a hospital or an orphanage, with no expectation of earthly reward. The reward sought from providing such services was "grace," or points toward getting into heaven. Martin Luther (1483–1546), a Catholic priest considered the father of the Protestant Reformation, declared that all work—be it building houses or working in the fields or making shoes—should be classified as good works, and considered worthy of grace because it contributed to the welfare of the community. He also legitimized the quest for profit, which the Catholic Church had deemed sinful, by deciding that the amount of profit one earned was a measure of how hard one had worked, and, therefore, of how much grace one deserved.

Owing largely to this change in philosophy, the middle class evolved. The citizens in this class were the businessmen. One of the prerequisites to succeeding as such was education. Primary producers, middlemen, and investors should be able to read, write, work with numbers, understand geography, and understand the law. Congregation members were encouraged to take greater control of their lives. Children were required to attend primary school so that the good of society might be served by the development of their potential.

The second reason, again, was technological. Quite simply, in 1445 Gutenberg built the first printing press. This invention eventually allowed printers to produce copies of documents and books at a rate and price that made the information and knowledge upon which education is based accessible to a much larger audience.

The next step, of course, now that education had begun shifting from the status of a privilege to that of a necessity, was to try to figure out how to provide it on a universal basis. Germany enacted Europe's first compulsory education laws in the mid-1500s. Other countries followed suit. The purpose of education during this period was two-fold. First, it was offered to make students better Christians, so The Bible and other religious passages were the major texts used in reading lessons. Second, it provided skills that allowed people to improve themselves economically.

2.2 Theoretical Roots of Modern Education

The following period in European history was the Enlightenment Period. With its tremendous optimism and its feet fixed firmly in the development ethic, the Enlightenment

Period gave us many important advances in education theory. A number of thinkers from different parts of Western Europe made important contributions. John Amos Comenius (1592–1670) of Austria is considered as the designer of our modern education system. He was one of the earliest champions of universal education. His contributions included the design of our current school hierarchy with kindergarten, elementary school, high school, college, and university components. He is considered the first to come up with the concept of educating each student according to his or her own nature and with the belief that students learn best through direct interaction with their environment. He developed what has evolved into the modern day textbook.

John Locke (1632–1704), considered as the father of liberalism or the right of individuals to shape their own values, carried the need to treat students as individuals even further, at least from a philosophical perspective. He said that children were products of their environment. He said that they begin as a "blank slate" on which the teacher writes, using reward and punishment to shape what the student retains. Locke said that the most powerful of such reward was enhancement of the student's self-esteem; he said that the most powerful punishment was the student's belief that he or she had disgraced him or herself. He said that teachers should be made responsible for building moral character as well as for providing subject matter, but that students should still enjoy the freedom to define their own values once mature enough and educated enough to make informed decisions.

Jean-Jacques Rousseau (1712–1778), a well-known Swiss philosopher, followed the lead of Comenius and Locke in terms of experiential learning. He focused on the need to respect individuality, especially when dealing with the very young. He believed that children were born good rather than in original sin. He fought the practice of forcing children to act like adults. Rousseau believed that moral education should not begin until children were old enough to reason effectively and that they should learn mainly through experience rather than through strict instruction, rote memorization, and indoctrination. Rousseau said that children should be allowed to be children before becoming adults; otherwise, their potential would not develop correctly and was in danger of being destroyed. These ideas were spelled out in his book, *Emile, or On Education* (1762), a book that was considered so radical that it was banned in certain quarters.

Rousseau was also a key figure in the Romanticism Movement that swept through Europe during this period. Emphasis was on individuals escaping the rigidity of logic and on individuals escaping the rigidity of rationalism with its dependence on reason. Emphasis was also on letting emotions and instinct direct behavior. Romanticism encouraged people to commune with nature when seeking truth. Benjamin Franklin, Thomas Jefferson, and John Adams carried the concept from the previously mentioned drawing rooms of France to the colonies where it became a foundational piece of our newly formed democracy. Romanticism fit well with the rugged individual, the self-made-man image of the American pioneer.

2.3 Opposing Schools of Thought Begin a Never-Ending Battle

Despite the arguments of educated men such as Comenius, Locke, and Rousseau that rose in support of using education as a vehicle to arouse curiosity concerning the world that students lived in and to develop individual potential, the prevailing pedagogical philosophy in Europe's education sector during the Enlightenment Period became that of John Calvin (1509–1564). Calvin was a French theologian and pastor who lived in Switzerland during the previous Protestant Reformation and played a large role in shaping it. Calvin believed and taught that man was born in sin and must work his way out of it, and that education was an important part of this process and should be forced on the young whether they desired it or not. He said that teachers should be stern and demanding, and that punishment should be severe for those who lagged in their studies because their behavior was miring them even more deeply in sin. He taught that memorization rather than understanding was the essence of a safe learning process. Calvin's philosophy shaped the European and North American colonies approach to education well into the late 1700s.

Johann Heinrich Pestalozzi (1746–1827), also a Swiss, joined Comenius, Locke, and Rousseau in refuting the fanatical demands of the Calvinists, supporting, instead, what was considered a radical perspective in terms of educating the young. Pestalozzi argued, like Locke, that rather than being collared with sin at birth, children were shaped by their environment. He argued that the key was to make their environment positive and supportive so that children could develop their positive potential. He said that education should be individualized, that each individual student's intuitions should be focused on, and that every aspect of the student's life should be taken into account. Pestalozzi argued that a comfortable home-like environment should exist at school. He argued that young children should use all their senses, that they should learn through their powers of observation rather than through abstract teaching, and that instruction should be based on everyday activities such as climbing stairs with the student counting the stairs as he or she climbed.

Pestalozzi argued that students should spend a lot of their school time in nature, and that they should use their senses as well as their minds and learn from natural materials found outside as well as from those brought into the classroom. He argued that students should be expected to express themselves verbally as part of the learning process, reporting accurately on what they had observed. Pestalozzi taught without books. He relied on students' manipulation of the objects presented for observation, and said that the instructor has to constantly interact with the students, "talking, questioning, explaining, and repeating." Finally, Pestaloozi argued that students should develop industrial skills—weaving, farming, and brick-laying—as well as academic skills.

Robert Owen (1771–1858) put Pestalozzi's theories into practice. Owen was an extremely successful industrialist, running the most successful cotton mill in Scotland. The management philosophy of most mill and manufactory owners during this period was to get the most productivity out of employees with the least possible reward. As a result, after adult male and female employees rebelled, children who could be more easily controlled and paid less were often brought in to work up to 14 hours a day at jobs that crippled and eventually killed them. Owen, guided by his own values and by Pestalozzi's theories on education, sought to change both the mill environment and culture using education for the young as his main vehicle. He tried to keep families together, all members working for the company. He said that children under the age of 10 should not work in the mill. He said that during their first 4 years of employment, young employees had to attend school. His system tried to turn learning into a positive process, rather than one driven by guilt and fear.

In 1815, Owen opened the first infant school at his mill. The students were children aged 1–6 whose parents worked there. The two people running the school were not professional teachers. They offered no formal subjects such as reading or arithmetic. Rather they taught informally through conversations, displays, projects, and field trips. In the early 1800s, Owen introduced his approach to education in the United States. He established a utopian community, New Harmony, in Indiana. Education was free to everybody in the community of any age, male or female. Learning was not accomplished through memorization, but was as hands-on as possible. For example, geography was taught by having students make their own maps; natural history included field trips so that students could see what they were learning about. Vocational training, which had been gained through on-the-job apprenticeships up to this point, was introduced for the first time as part of a school's curriculum. Although New Harmony and its novel approach to learning were short-lived (three years), the effort provided a model for later advances and reforms in the U.S. education system.

Meanwhile, back in France, The Emperor Napoleon Bonaparte (1769–1821) was instituting a strong, centralized system that provided universal education, at least for males. He divided France into districts, each with its own school. He designed curriculum for these schools. He excluded the Church from any involvement. One of his major objectives in designing and building the system was to educate all male French citizens so that they would be better prepared to rule the world once he and his armies had conquered it.

Across the channel in England, at the same time, the fact that both the French and British systems did not accept women students bothered Mary Wollstonecraft (1759–1797), one of the period's leading advocates for women's rights. In reaction she wrote a piece entitled: *A Vindication of the Rights of Women*, arguing that women should be men's "intellectual companions," that they should be well enough educated to support themselves, and that they should receive access to equal opportunity in terms of schooling. She wrote that, "… expectations for women and for men should be equal." She envisioned a society in which "the qualities of an individual, rather than their sex would determine what they would do and how they would be treated" (Button, p. 70).

Although a growing number of nations began to realize the benefits of universal education, opposition to it remained strong, especially in Great Britain. Despite Robert Owen's successes, and despite Wollstonecraft's protests, industrial leaders tried to block efforts to provide primary and secondary education not only for women but for poor, working-class males, and for children. The Reverend Thomas Malthus (1766–1834), a revered spokesman for the industrialists, helped rationalize this viewpoint by blaming poverty on the poor, saying that the poor were lazy, not at all thrifty, and spent their spare time creating new mouths to feed. He was against supporting them in any way. He said that whenever the economy improved, population figures also rose among the poor, absorbing the new profits so that society suffered. He said that the only solution was to keep the poor at work for longer hours so that they were too tired to create new babies. This included keeping poor children at work so that they did not fall victim to and become accustomed to the follies of idleness that caused such suffering.

The result of Malthus' attitude was a work week that stretched to 14–15 hours a day, 6 days a week for children as young as five and six. The result was an average life expectancy in some industrial areas of 18 years, such expectancy not exceeding 30 anywhere that people spent most of their hours in manufactories. Malthus said that the working class did not need education to do what they were born to do. Also, he said that education was dangerous for laborers in that it might lead them to question the system, causing disturbances that hampered the production process and the generation of wealth.

As late as the 1850s, Sir Charles Adderley, given responsibility for Great Britain's education policy, refused to budge on the issue of universal education. He defended the *status quo* by declaring that, "it is clearly wrong to keep ordinary children of the working class at school after the age at which their proper work begins (five, maybe six?)." To do so "would be as arbitrary and improper as it would be to keep the boys attending Eton and Harrow at spade labour" (Bryson, 2010, p. 414). A number of historians believe that the country's refusal to provide education for the masses, a decision not in keeping with what was going on throughout the rest of Europe, was at least partly responsible for the decline of the British Empire.

2.4 A Dilemma Faced by Educators

The efforts of these early shapers of educational philosophy eventually brought them face-to-face with a previously mentioned dilemma that we continue to struggle with today; one we now need to explore in greater depth, the dilemma of whether society should concentrate on generating an education system that encourages entire classes of students to master standardized offerings, or whether it should generate one that focuses on allowing each student to realize and enjoy his or her individual potential to the fullest possible extent as Comenius and Pestalozzi advocated. Doing both in a school or class of any size was impossible. The number of students involved even then was usually too large. At the same time, the slow-to-evolve stream of classroom-process-assisting technology has never been up to the challenge.

As a result, while our desire was to do it all, we were forced by both social and mechanical constraints to focus on bringing the class as a whole up to a specified level of learning. Moreover, that problem intensified during the Industrial Revolution (roughly 1750 to modern times in Europe; roughly 1850 to modern times in the United States). European cities were flooded with immigrants from the countryside looking for jobs in the new manufactories, most of them having lost their work in the fields to new farming technology. U.S. cities were eventually flooded by immigrants from European nations, and by other people seeking a better life. During this period, government systems and the public education system it supported were dominated by powerful industrialists whose primary objective was to turn these new employees into workers capable of functioning productively in factories. To do so, the workers now needed to function as a complement the new, rapidly improving technology. Managerial emphasis was on standardizing technology so that it would produce standardized products. In order for workers to fit efficiently into the process, therefore, they needed to be standardized as well. So, out the window went emphasis on individual potential.

Since the main purpose of the school system was now to feed standardized students into the standardized workplace so that things would run smoothly and the desired growth could continue unabated, societies tried to move as many students as possible toward the desired norm.

The growth ethic mentality that evolved during the early Industrial Revolution to replace the development ethic mentality of the Enlightenment Period reinforced this focus. In the growth ethic workplace, emphasis was on efficiency of production, on cutting down the number of steps required, the amount of time required, the number of parts required, and the number of rejects. Efficiency was, in turn, dependent on the standardization of equipment, of procedures, of management practices, and of employees.

In the classroom, in order to meet such requirement, societies developed a pedagogy that moved as many students as possible as quickly as possible in the right direction. We ran our schools much like traditional assembly-line factories. At the same time, in the name of efficiency, we too often discouraged uniqueness. It slowed things down and hindered us in attempts to meet our quota of standardized students.

Leadership in the Industrial Revolution era classroom was also modeled on leadership in the Industrial Revolution workshop. An adversarial relationship frequently existed between the teacher (boss) and students (workers). The teacher (boss) made all the important decisions with no input from the students (workers). The students (workers) were responsible to the teacher (boss) for satisfactorily completing a predefined quantity of work in a predefined amount of time. Their reward (grades) was based on their production level.

A strict hierarchy existed in the classroom mirroring that in the workplace. Boundaries of authority were well defined and guarded. Team efforts were relatively rare, and students (workers) were in no way encouraged to help improve their coworkers' (classmates') performance. In fact, they were usually in competition with classmates (coworkers) and could improve their situation only at the expense of these people because the teacher (boss) was grading on a curve. Only so many "A"s ($4 per hour), "B"s ($3 per hour), and "C"s ($2 per hour) were awarded. The rationalization in the classroom as in the workplace was that such competition inspired students (workers) to try harder.

2.5 Rationalizations That Don't Work

Money is the reward in the growth-ethic-driven workplace. The amount of money produced by society, however, is always limited. As a result, we must decide how best to divide it. Not everyone can earn as much as they want. Therefore, we force employees to compete for it, the "scarcity mentality" coming into play. The scarcity mentality arises when not enough of an important resource, in this case money, exists to satisfy everyone's needs and desires. Those "without" try to win it away from those "with." At the same time, owing to the possibility of losing what they already have, those "with" continue to stockpile it even after all needs are satisfied as a hedge against lost.

In the education sector, the number of "A"s available takes the place of the amount of money available in the workplace. This number is also limited. There are not enough "A"s for everyone to earn one. Therefore, we must force students to compete for them, to struggle against each other for them.

This analogy between money and grades, however, is incorrect. It is based on a false, although convenient, assumption. In terms of the falseness, while owing to its nature and role, there will always be limits to the amount of money generated, knowledge is different. There will never be natural limits to the amount of knowledge available to individuals, be it the same knowledge that currently exists and is shared without anyone losing anything, or a more progressed level of knowledge that can be generated and made available for consumption. In fact, quite the opposite is true—the more knowledge we generate, the more we make possible.

When students learn something, therefore, it does not reduce the amount others can learn. Rather, it usually has the opposite effect and increases that amount. As a result of this reality, competition in the area of education is unnecessary at best, antithetical to success at worst. Hence, teachers should obviously be working to award as many "A"s ($4 per hour) as possible in order to strengthen the system and speed up the spread of development enhancing knowledge.

However, that is not the way it works in our traditional education sector. The growth ethic mentality approach of forcing students to compete for grades is too convenient as a means of dividing them up into the necessary workplace categories. There can be so many CEOs, executives, middle managers, hourly workers, and so many janitors. Therefore, we should pass out only so many "A"s, "B"s, "C"s, and "D"s.

There is, of course, guilt associated with this strategy. Teachers know deep down that these parameters are, at best, a very superficial measure of potential. Apologists, therefore, have been forced to come up with an appropriate rationalization. That rationalization is a statistical tool—the famous Bell-Shaped Density Curve. The Bell-Shaped Density Curve provides a convenient breakdown of student potential which, to no one's surprise, very neatly fits the needs of the growth-ethic culture workplace. It shows statistically that, on the average, student populations do, indeed, vary in potential—a few at the top of the scale, a whole lot in the middle, and a few at the bottom. Moreover, it has the numbers to prove what it is saying, lots of numbers, thousands of numbers, and millions of numbers.

This thousands of numbers and millions of numbers bit, however, is the problem. The Bell-Shaped Density Curve, we discover, was developed as a means of showing the density at various points in a range defining the variance of one characteristic in a large population, be it natural, mechanical, or human. The Curve was first described in 1733 by a man named De Moivre, and then rediscovered a half century later by astronomers named Laplace and Gauss, who used it to describe the behavior of errors in astronomical measurements.

In terms of the social sciences, the Curve says that if you plot the measured amount of one characteristics—say intelligence—in thousands of students, the individual data points representing that characteristic, when charted on a scale, should create such a curve with roughly 20% at the high end, 60% in the middle, and 20% at the low end, though there can be variations.

What it definitely does not say, however, is that the scholastic abilities of students in an individual class, in an individual school, when plotted on a graph, create the same curve. For one thing, the concept has never been proven. It is a phenomenon that sometimes occurs when a large number of data points are analyzed. For another thing, without exception, the concept is not valid when involving a relatively small number of subjects.

Also, one of the things the Bell-Shaped Density Curve approach is incapable of taking into account is the "purposefulness" of human beings, a concept explained by Russell Ackoff and Fred Emery in their book *On Purposeful Systems*. The definition of "purposeful" in this context is that people can define their own objectives and their own ways of achieving these objectives. They are also capable of changing both their objectives and their ways of achieving them when they want to, which means that if students are given the right incentive, if they are inspired, they can improve their performance.

Finally, when creating a Bell-Shaped Density Curve for student performance we cannot take into account the difference in the ability of teachers. One teacher might be excellent in teaching math, for example, and have the whole class doing

"A"- and "B"-level work. Another might not really like teaching math and have the whole class doing "C"-level work. Yet, the demands of the Curve force both to give out roughly the same number of "A"s, "B"s, and "C"s.

What academia has done, in effect, is to misuse an unproven statistical tool, the Bell-Shaped Density Curve, in order to excuse practices it believes important to the success of an economic system driven by the growth ethic. By doing so, however, academia has made it even more difficult to focus on the development of individual potential, which situation causes a whole lot of teachers to be unhappy. But because society does not know how to resolve the involved dilemma, it spends time and energy trying to patch up and make acceptable the current model.

Evidence of this misguided effort is the modern day concern with grade inflation. The inference is that the Curve is still valid, but that teachers are getting soft. I have found very few articles challenging this assumption, articles suggesting, instead, that teachers might be getting better, that students might be getting smarter. I have found very few articles suggesting that as our focus shifts toward the realization of individual ability and potential—toward the development ethic—continued dependence on the Bell-Shaped Density Curve in the individual classroom and school setting is counter-productive.

2.6 Good Intentions Lead to Naught

It's not that teachers aren't trying. Let me tell a story that certainly fits here. We have the pleasure of knowing a young man named Ray who is a high school English teacher. Ray had a habit of sitting at his desk at the start of a semester picking out the "A-," "B-," and "C"-level students as they filed in. It was 11th grade; by that time, students had been pretty well slotted.

Eventually, Ray said, he had grown uneasy with this practice. It was too mechanical; it was unfair. It wasn't what teaching was all about, or should be all about. So Ray made a decision. At the beginning of the following semester, he stood up and announced that no one in the class would be allowed to earn less than an "A." The students had been surprised, to say the least. There followed some nervous laughter, just in case it was a joke. Ray had continued by explaining how this new approach was going to be managed. He would assign reports and creative pieces to be written. He would give tests. If students received less than an "A," they would be required to make an appointment with him, go over the material, rewrite the paper, or retake the test, and to continue doing so until the "A" was earned.

Two weeks later the first required paper was handed back. About one-third of the class received "A"s. Ray told the rest of his students to make an appointment with him during a study hall or after school. Some complained, but eventually they all made their appointments. About half earned their "A"s the second time around. Ray handed the papers back and told the rest to make an appointment. By this time, the students realized he was serious and buckled down.

From that point on, Ray said, the level of class enthusiasm grew steadily. Students who were traditionally silent or distracted began taking part. A "C" student who was forced to rework his poem three times entered it into a local college competition and had it read as a winning entry. Also, an unexpected thing occurred. Now that the competition for grades was gone, some of the better students began helping others with their reworking to ease the load on Ray.

By the end of the semester, the atmosphere in the class was, to say the least, positive. A number of students had realized they were capable of a lot more than they had previously thought. Almost all had expanded their horizons.

Happy ending? Maybe in a society driven by the development ethic, but in one based on our current growth ethic mentality I'm afraid that Ray never really had a chance. He soon had to stop following his conscience and go back to teaching the old way. The first shot came when our young acquaintance was called to the principal's office. He assumed that he was going to receive praise for his innovative approach. Instead, when he arrived, the principle chastised him, for—you guessed it—grade inflation. The old Bell-Shaped Density Curve had struck again. Bad for the reputation of the school, the principle explained; state examiners would begin asking uncomfortable questions.

The second shot came when several parents from the honor roll set called to protest. Their children had worked hard and done well according to the rules. But their achievements meant less now. On paper, at least in Ray's course, they looked just the same as the ones who had struggled. Colleges wouldn't take their academic records seriously because everyone in the class had the same grade. It wasn't fair, the parents said. And, in a growth ethic mentality society with its emphasis on competition, on "winning," the parents were right; it really wasn't fair.

The third reason was that the effort, no matter how noble, consumed too much time. Ray spent hours with these individual students, frequently after school, which interfered with his other teaching responsibilities; which caused parents, coaches, employers, and others to complain; which threw his own life schedule completely out of whack.

Finally, the fourth reason, which also had to do with time and teaching responsibilities, was that owing to his focus on the lower end of the student spectrum in terms of releasing potential, he had been able to spend less time with his stars. They had gained something from helping their struggling classmates, but not as much as if he had been able to spend more time with them individually, guiding and encouraging their efforts.

Chapter 3

Education in the United States during the Colonial Period

3.1 Breaking with European Tradition

The early colonies in what is now the United States were mostly made up of people from Great Britain, a large number having been driven out as a result of their religious beliefs, many seeking wealth, some exiled as criminals or individuals who had fallen into disfavor with the authorities. Still, however, they were British and brought with them the British tradition. One example of this was the caste system. Society in the colonies was divided roughly into five castes. The clergy along with those wealthy enough to own land constituted the upper, governing class. The next level included skilled artisans; then unskilled laborers; then indentured servants; and, finally, the lowest class, slaves.

The early settlers also brought across the Atlantic the European focus on education as a means of strengthening the church and the religious character of citizens, as a vehicle for making them better Christians. During the 1600s Europe was immersed in the Protestant Reformation and labored under the previously mentioned Calvinist doctrines of predetermination, of man being born in sin and needing to spend the rest of his or her life struggling for redemption. One path to such redemption was through reading and memorizing passages from the Bible. Obviously, one first had to learn to read, so that reading was the original subject taught both in Great Britain and in the colonies, often to the exclusion of all others.

Religious fanaticism shaped both governance and education in the early colonies. While the Puritans had been driven out of England as a result of intolerance, once established in the "new world" they themselves became even less tolerant. Early education was shaped by such fervor. Students were expected to do exactly as they were told without question. They read what they were told to read, and memorized exactly what they were told to memorize. The *New England Primer* that "taught millions to read and not one to sin" was used in colonial schools for over 100 years. Typical passages included, "In Adam's fall we sinned all."; "Peter denies his Lord and cries."; and "The idle fool is whipt at school." (Noble, 1954, p. 27).

While Great Britain's curriculum was eventually enriched to cover the literary contributions of Shakespeare, Ben Jonson, Francis Bacon, Milton, and others, the colonies, owing largely to the influence of the Puritans and other strict religious communities, stayed with the Bible and sermons, thus missing out on the great burst of literary brilliance and scientific discovery that was occurring not only in Britain but all over Western Europe. Sir Isaac Newton defined the role of gravity; Robert Boyle identified laws that explained the pressures exerted by gases. Descartes, Leibnitz, and Nader were making major contributions in the field of mathematics. William Harvey was studying blood circulation in the body.

A majority of the early colonists ignored the advances being made abroad, because such advances too frequently contradicted the strict religious beliefs that colonial culture was built around. Anyways, education was not *a priority* for most. It was mainly for the upper levels of the caste system. The rest of the population was too busy trying to survive. As a result, before the year 1700, an estimated 75% of the women and 50% of the men living in the colonies were illiterate. For those who did receive schooling, it was received in the home or, if one was an apprentice, from the family that owned the business (Noble, 1954, p. 7).

As education gradually became more formalized, each community set its own standards and its own curriculum. Some wealthier families brought tutors over from Europe. Most instructors, however, were home grown, largely self-educated, and self-trained in the art of teaching. Emphasis remained on reading, but eventually writing skills, speaking skills, and basic arithmetic were added. Women were allowed to learn only the scriptures, anything else being considered too dangerous. Teaching students to use reason and logic was not a consideration. Neither was the identification nor was the exploration of individual student interests. In fact, such learnings were considered as pathways to temptation and further sin. Emphasis remained on religious training, and the failure of students to stay on track often resulted in severe corporal punishment.

3.2 How Students Learned

School-based education during this period began with a study of the alphabet. Each student would be given a "hornbook" that consisted of a sheet of paper or transparent horn shellacked to a wooden paddle. On the sheet of paper was printed the alphabet, the Lord's Prayer, the benediction, and perhaps a brief religious warning. Students would start by memorizing the alphabet. Then they would learn syllables. Once students could recognize words, they progressed to the Bible and other religious readings (Noble, 1954, pp. 26–27). Emphasis, however, was on being able to read and repeat the words rather than on understanding their meaning based on one's personal perception. The church took the responsibility of providing such understanding. Writing and mathematics were eventually introduced, but these subjects were taught at a different school.

During the mid-1600s laws were passed in several colonies requiring that children be taught to read as a means of saving their souls. The first such law was designed by the Massachusetts colony in 1642. It called for the appointment of officials to investigate the ability of all children to read and to understand "the principles of religion and the capital laws for the country." (Cubberley, 1934, p. 16). In 1647, Massachusetts then passed a second law requiring mandatory schooling for all children at the primary level. This law was enacted in an attempt to foil the efforts of the "old deluder Satan" to restrain people from gaining the knowledge of scriptures necessary to salvation.

Two types of schools were in place by that time. The first was a "reading and writing school" that provided the basics for those in apprenticeships so they would become good, well-read Christians who would obey the law, obey their masters, and who would be able to contribute to the growth of the economy. The second was the "Latin grammar school" that prepared students for college and for leadership positions.

The primary content of reading and writing school instruction was religious and moral. Memorization, along with blind acceptance of what students were told by the instructor, was required. Numbers were also taught, their principle purpose in this context being to help students find "any chapter, Psalm, or verse in the Bible" (Spring, 1994, p. 11).

Latin grammar schools, in order to fill their charter, concentrated on the study of Latin grammar, Latin conversation and composition, and Latin readings, the language being necessary for religious studies, for the study of medicine, and for the reading of the classics. Students also studied Greek grammar and literature and, sometimes, Hebrew grammar. Mornings at the typical Latin grammar school during this period were devoted to grammar, afternoons to literature, Fridays to review and testing, Saturdays and Sundays to religious themes (Cremin, 1970, p. 15).

The first such school, opened in Boston in the year 1635, was catering, as has been said, mainly to young men in their teens from families belonging to the social elite. The movement then spread across the colonies, and schools gradually expanded the scope of what they offered. Latin grammar schools were supported by tuition from families with money, by farm produce, by funds from wealthy contributors, sometimes by monies from the community treasury.

3.3 Getting the Framework into Place

Harvard, the first college created in the colonies, was founded in 1636 with monies provided by the Massachusetts legislature along with a gift from the Puritan minister, John Harvard, which included his library of some 260 volumes. The college's original purpose was to produce trained clergy well versed in Latin and the classics. The group behind the project included several graduates of Oxford and Cambridge who had immigrated to the colonies and wanted to establish an educational institution modeled on their alma maters. The college's first president, Henry Dunster, who was also frequently its sole instructor, battled continually with local religious leaders over what the most appropriate curriculum should include. By 1650, the school's charter had changed to include the study of all good literature, of the arts, and of the sciences (Button and Provenzo, 1989, p. 28).

The pattern for those who chose to pursue formal learning, then, at least in the Massachusetts colony which, at that point, was the most progressive in terms of education, was home schooling in reading and writing by parents, siblings, or tutors followed by six or seven years of Latin grammar school for boys in families doing well enough financially to avoid putting them immediately into apprenticeships. While these schools frequently consisted of only one instructor, other instructors could be contracted to teach subjects, including geography, mathematics, and history. The availability of these other instructors was sometimes advertised in the local newspaper. Control over the Latin grammar school system varied, decisions concerning them sometimes being made during town meetings; sometimes by a committee; sometimes by tuition payers; even by the involved teachers, or "masters," as they were called. Finally, for the financial and intellectual elite, three years were spent at Harvard.

The late 1600s and early 1700s were part of the previously mentioned Enlightenment Period, perhaps, in terms of conceptual development, the most productive period in western history. The foundations of European and, eventually, U.S. culture were defined and put firmly into place during this era. Prior to this time the masses had no real voice in government. But in the 1700s, men such as John Locke, Jean Jacques Rousseau, and Thomas Jefferson refuted this practice, saying that all men are created equal. These Enlightenment thinkers believed that all citizens, no matter what their station, should be involved in shaping government policies and decisions. To do so wisely, however, they needed access to education. Thus, rather than a privilege enjoyed only by the upper classes, education gradually became a right required for all.

The North American colonialists also took to reading during the Enlightenment Period, absorbing the classics from their mother continent. By 1750, the works of European thinkers could be found on the bookstands of many colonial cities. Local printing presses began turning out newspapers, almanacs, tracts, and sermons exploring current politics, advances in science, as well as religious and philosophical issues. Those running the presses had shaken off the restrictions originally placed on them by religious leaders and begun both feeding and leading public conversation on a wide range of topics. News journals filled with commentary were published. Thousands of copies of newspapers were sold, Benjamin Franklin's the *Pennsylvania Gazette* (1729) becoming the most popular, enjoying distribution in several of the colonies.

Franklin is also credited for opening the first "academy" in the United States, a private institution that focused on delivering a more comprehensive education, including the study of Latin, Greek, and English languages as well as French, German, and Spanish. To this list of subjects, he added history, physics, geography, chronology, logic, rhetoric, writing, arithmetic, algebra, geometry, science, bookkeeping, and drawing as emphasis in the education sector continued to shift from theological training to "studies that will be useful in approaching the active scenes of life." Franklin then broke these studies down into three separate schools—the English school, the Latin school, and the mathematical school—offering a different combination of courses in each, thus providing a model for our present day secondary school and college/university tracking system (Button, p. 47).

In terms of educating the general public, Franklin opened the first library accessible to all. In 1727, he formed a club called the "Junto," a group of men who met weekly to discuss philosophical, moral, and political issues. Members were requested to present and defend an individual essay once every three months. The members eventually pooled their books to form the first subscription library, patrons paying a fee for access that helped cover library expenses and made possible the purchase of new books. By 1763, more than 23 libraries had been established in the colonies to serve the general public.

Prior to the Revolutionary War, eight other institutions of higher learning besides Harvard were established to educate future clergy. These included William and Mary and the rest of the Ivy League schools. All but two of the latter—Columbia University and the University of Pennsylvania—were established by different Protestant religions to train ministers. Very quickly, however, they too strayed, influenced to a large degree by their more sophisticated European counterparts, and began offering more practical subject matter as well.

3.4 Others Who Helped Shape the Colonial Education System

Another major contributor to the form and philosophy of our current education system was Thomas Jefferson (1743–1826). Following the Revolutionary War, the main concern of the nation's founding fathers was to discover the best balance between freedom and order. Most of them emphasized the need for order, partially owing to their desire to maintain the *status quo* in terms of class, to maintain their position as the elite. Jefferson was one of the few to argue that freedom of opportunity came first, in order for the nation to live up to the promises made in its constitution, and that equal educational opportunity should be enjoyed by all.

Jefferson based this position on his belief that the backbone, the strength of a democracy lay in its education system, that universal education was necessary to survival, and "that such a system must provide its citizens with the understanding and knowledge necessary for them to not only pursue their own personal happiness, but also fulfill their obligations and duties as citizens" (Button, p. 67). He believed that the most important area of study, once the required level of expertise in reading, writing, and arithmetic had been achieved, was history. Reading the newspaper daily and studying history were the only other activities required for the preparation of students to become good citizens with high moral values, the study of history teaching them what was right and what was wrong.

Jefferson believed that the education system should help identify and train future leaders. He proposed that an intellectual aristocracy should emerge that would stand beside the one based on wealth and pedigree. He intended to help create this intellectual aristocracy through the formation of a school system with three tiers. On the first tier, every citizen, male and female, would, in reading and writing schools, receive at least three years of reading, writing, mathematics, and civics. The second tier of Jefferson's educational hierarchy would include already existing Latin grammar schools and academies similar to Benjamin Franklin's that families would pay to send their sons to. The best among the reading and writing school students whose families could not afford the expense of further education would receive publicly funded scholarships to a Latin grammar school or academy.

After six years of education at this level, each class would be divided in terms of academic achievement. The lower half would find jobs, frequently as instructors teaching at Latin grammar schools or at academies. The upper half would continue on to college for three more years at public expense. Jefferson was against any sort of religious indoctrination in his system. To reinforce this, he said that no clergy should be allowed to hold administrative positions in the school system, though religion would be accepted as a field of study. He was also against use of the education system to shape political values, though, as has been said, he strongly supported its role in the shaping of future leaders.

Concerning the classroom process, Jefferson is best known for his *Seven Keys of Great Teaching,* which include, "Classics, not Textbooks"; "Mentors, not Professors"; "Inspire, not Require"; "Structure Time, not Content"; "Quality, not Conformity"; "Simplicity, not Complexity"; and "You, not Them." Most of these keys still make good sense today (Feldman and Benjamin, 2006, p. 321).

As a student himself, Jefferson had become well versed in the literature of ancient Greece. He had obviously studied Aristotle's works. He was familiar with the development ethic, which is probably the source for what he said about citizens "pursuing their own personal happiness while fulfilling their obligations and duties as citizens" (Button, p. 67). Jefferson also obviously had Aristotle's teachings in mind when he wrote *The Declaration of Independence*. "We hold these truths to be self-evident, that all men are created equal, that they are endowed by their Creator with certain unalienable rights, that among these are life, liberty and the pursuit of happiness." The definition of "happiness" in this instance concerned the practice of "moral virtue" in the act of governance (Aristotle's dimension of "doing"); virtuous governance being that which allowed and encouraged the development of individual positive potential.

Finally, Jefferson most likely had these teachings in mind when he designed the school system to encourage what Aristotle defined as life's primary dimension of "knowing." He tried to find the model that provided the greatest opportunity for the greatest number. In order to provide education for the entire public, Jefferson called in 1779 for Virginia counties to be divided into school districts, each district supporting a school open to all children that would offer a uniform curriculum and provide three years of free education. His effort failed mainly because of growing class consciousness, but in 1785 and 1787, owing in large part to his lobbying and influence, the new U.S. Federal Government passed laws supporting the establishment of primary and secondary "common schools" and providing states with funds to buy land on which to locate them. The government did not, however, provide funds to support these common schools once established. That was left up to the states, which were not collecting enough taxes at that point to do so. As a result, the burden was passed on down to the community, the communities frequently turning to lotteries as a major source of the required funding.

Besides Franklin and Jefferson, one other person whose contribution stood out during this period was Benjamin Rush, a physician who, along with Franklin and Jefferson, was also a signer of the Declaration of Independence. Rush believed that the current education system with its loose network of independent reading and writing schools, Latin grammar schools, and academies, each shaping its own curriculum, was encouraging diversity rather than the desired uniformity of thought. He sought to encourage the latter. Rush, however, unlike Jefferson, wanted to make religion a major component of the education curriculum, believing that on-going training in the principles of Christianity would create better citizens. Rush was also a strong advocate for the education of women, believing that they should receive most of the academic training now received by men.

In early colonial days, as had been said, very few women were encouraged to learn to read or write. These skills, along with arithmetic, were required to run a business and men ran the businesses. The role of women was to raise children, to take care of the home, tend the garden, weave cloth, and prepare food. They learned what they needed to know from their mothers. However, at least in upper class families, women were also responsible for educating their young male offspring. Obviously, they first need to find some way of learning what was required themselves, doing so quietly.

Men were also the only family members allowed to vote (if they were property owners). So the men took part in politics, reading the newspaper and political tracts. This situation changed little until the United States won its independence from Great Britain. At that point, the realization came that women needed to play a greater role in generating a stable and patriotic society. Established academies began accepting female students. Also, new schools were opened that accepted only young women and taught all the subjects offered in the original academies. Many of the graduates of these schools went into teaching, the first profession into which woman practitioners were welcomed. Then, in 1819, the first womens' teaching school, The Troy Female Seminary, was opened in New York offering as an incentive "instruction on credit," students paying their tuition after graduating and finding jobs.

The philosophy that drove the Enlightenment Period found its roots in the pronouncement by the scientist, Sir Isaac Newton (1642–1727) that the universe resembled a large clock. Newton said that the clock had been started by God, but that once running, the laws of physics kept it going. Enlightenment thinkers believed that because the universe was governed by the same laws of physics governing a clock, once these laws were understood scientists could ferret out all the secrets of the universe. Ultimately, because our reality was contained within the universe, the vehicle of science would eventually allow us to develop an understanding of every part of that reality.

In the world of scholarship, as a result of this thinking and enthusiasm, emphasis began gradually to shift from the production of submissive students who memorized passages and blindly absorb dictations to students who appreciated and strove for freedom of thought and discovery. Benjamin Franklin's academy and those modeled on it exposed students to an expanding range of subjects and focused increasingly on the practical skills. These academies also broke seriously from the traditional domination of education by religion. Robart Molesworth wrote in 1692 that "in order to contribute to liberty and freedom, education must be secular and sepa-rate from religion, that professors should replace priests as teachers, and that students should focus on understanding the content of the classical studies rather than on understanding the grammar" (Molesworth, 1976, p. 56).

Following the Revolutionary War another major debate arose. This one was about whether the education system should be used to instill patriotism in students or whether, as Thomas Jefferson had proposed, it should stay away from political education, focusing solely on providing the tools and techniques necessary to the formation of political opinions. Those who supported using the system to instill patriotism were influenced by the challenge of unifying a population that included original colonists along with more recent immigrants from England, Germany, France, Holland, and Africa as well as Native Americans. By 1766, for example, the population of the state of Pennsylvania was roughly one-third English, one-third German, and one-third a mix of other nationalities (Spring, 1994, p. 16). How do officials combine these cultures into one? Which cultural flavor should be dominant? Since the new nation had begun as part of the British Empire, because most of the leaders of the new nation had British roots, a movement began to make English the official language of the education sector, the government, and the economy.

One of the leaders of this movement was the Connecticut-born schoolmaster Noah Webster (1758–1843) best known for *Webster's Dictionary*, an updated version of which is still in use. Webster, however, also published an "American" version of the Bible as well as a spelling-book–grammar-book–reader combination that eventually sold over 75 million copies and helped shape U.S. education policy for nearly a century (Spring, 1994, p. 55). The text found in his publications encouraged patriotism and Christianity. Webster, being a disciple of John Locke's blank slate theory of education, believed that children had to be taught these things, and that they had to be conditioned through the education process to be good American citizens and good Christians.

Chapter 4

Education in the United States during the Early 1800s

4.1 The Scattershot Approach

By the early 1800s, with the exception of Franklin-style academies and some private schools, little had actually changed in terms of subject matter and teaching pedagogy. No standardization of curriculum existed in the government-supported supposedly universal network of common schools so that each individual teacher—and there was usually only one—did his or her own thing, focusing on the basics—reading, spelling, writing, and sometimes arithmetic. Another problem during this period was the fact that 80% of the population still lived in a rural setting, spread across the countryside. So, which was the best location for the common school established to serve these children? Also, schools were open only periodically. In northern states weather frequently forced their closure during the winter. In summer, planting and harvesting took precedence in all states.

Students usually provided their own books. Because not many texts had been published at that point, the few existing ones were used in most schools across the new nation. They represented the first possibility for standardization though, no syllabi existed at that time and instructors made use of the included material in any manner they chose.

Teachers were also scarce and trained teachers were rare, partially because before the 1900s they didn't earn very much. Upon arriving in a community, a master would announce the subjects that he or she was able to teach and the fee for services in an *article of agreement*, which was passed through the community gathering to obtain signatures from families that wished to enroll their children. Usually, as part of the salary, the parents of students would provide a free bed and meals. This practice was called "boarding round." The teacher spends a week or more in the home of each student, then, gathering up his or her belongings, moves onto the next home.

Another reason that the United States continued to lag in its educational efforts was that at the beginning of the 1800s, though leaders in the economic sector were becoming excited about the potential of technology, by reports of industrialization occurring in European nations, the U.S.'s economy continued to be based primarily on agriculture. The Industrial Revolution that was reshaping European culture had not yet gained real momentum in the U.S. Formal education; therefore, was not considered important many communities preferring to pay fines to the state government rather than to open a mandated common school.

For the wealthy, for those families that did consider education important, a growing number of academies were chartered by state governments, first for men, then also for young ladies, more than 1000 by the year 1830. Many of them, including Phillips Exeter and Phillips Andover, are still operating today and continue to cater to the wealthy. As the number of private schools continued to grow, parents who paid for their children's private education began to balk at supporting common schools and began competing for government funds. Their argument was four-fold: (1) The additional tax burden was unfair for those already paying for private school. (2) Education was wasted on lower-class students who would make little use of it. (3) The public schools did not include religions training as part of their offering. (4) A successful public sector would break down class distinctions, reducing everyone to the same level of mediocricy (Cubberley, 1934, pp. 165–166).

4.2 Educating the Poor

Meanwhile, on the economic front, the major objective of those designing new technology and improving old was to facilitate the production of wagons or rifles or pairs of shoes or ships. Continuing efforts were made to increase the involved efficiencies. One of the ways to do so was to group into one building all the machines necessary for turning out a complete product; another was to group a large number of same machine manufacturing and the same product together in order to encourage economies of scale. This efficiency-increasing move led to the birth of the "manufactory" movement.

Machines soon became society's best friend. A rapidly growing school of managerial thought believed that the closer the cultures could model their social systems on machines, the more productive these systems would be. One of the social systems talked about was education. During the early 1800s the belief grew in the United States that properly organized educational institutions could solve the problems of society and perfect the human character. For the poor they would supplement or replace a weak family structure. As a result of this belief, "charity schools" for the public, frequently supported at least partially by churches or other private organizations, were opened in depressed city neighborhoods to administer to the moral ailments of the poor.

The Lancastrian System was developed to provide education for the rapidly growing number of students eligible for charity schools. Where it was instituted, the involved schools were referred to as "machines of great potential," efficient at producing the desired outcome, every student functioning as a cog to be honed to the required specifications.

With the Lancaster System, older, more advance students taught small groups of younger students. The idea was obviously modeled on the apprenticeship system in the workplace. Probably since the earliest days of mankind, those with skills as craftsmen shared their skills, training younger family members or, eventually, during the days of the guild system, training outsiders. Charity schools using the Lancaster System were popular with the taxpayers because they were relatively cheap to operate, students rather than professionals doing most of the teaching.

The older students who functioned as monitors received their instruction from the master who was a legitimate teacher and sat at the head of the class. Groups of students would be assigned one or several monitors who sat in the same row with them. The students would march back and forth in their row receiving integrated instruction from their monitors. The rewards for these students were prizes they competed for, most of their assignments involving rote memorization. The student who memorized the most won the prize.

The Lancaster System was the first education system to be compared to an assembly-line manufacturing process. An individual teacher with the assistance of monitors could handle and education several hundred students at a time.

At the other end of the economic spectrum, the children of more fortunate families attended a growing number of private schools. The movement toward universal public education, however, could not be stopped. James G. Carter (1795–1840), a Massachusetts state legislator, helped establish the first State

Board of Education in the United States, then began the first "normal school," a school where future teachers were trained. Students would enter normal schools directly upon finishing their education in a common school, spend one or two years studying, then begin their careers.

By 1900, despite Carter's efforts, less than half of the teachers working at the common school level had received this additional education. For most of them, continuing education following graduation from normal school was limited to attendance of conferences sponsored once or twice a year by teacher institutes. During these conferences, sessions on the theory and practice of education were supposedly delivered, though the major emphasis is reported to have frequently been on strengthening the moral character of attendants so that they could provide a role model for students. Some have compared these teacher institute sessions to old-time revival meetings.

4.3 Horace Mann Makes the Common School System a Serious Player

The U.S. common school education system until the mid-1800s remained a loose network of independent institutions, each pretty much so doing its own thing, supporting itself, fielding its own curriculum. The network had been put into place by this time, but that was about it in terms of successful organization. A major turning point came when in 1837 Horace Mann (1796–1859) became the first head of Massachusetts' State Board of Education and decided it time to take public education in his state seriously. At that juncture some 3000 common schools existed in Massachusetts, "each being governed by its own habits, traditions, and local customs with no common, superintending power over them, no bond of brotherhood … if any improvement in principles or modes of teaching is discovered by talent or accident in one school, instead of being published to the world, it dies with the discoverer" (Cremin, 1980, p. 155).

Mann was born into a strict Calvinist family and culture. At a young age, however, he rebelled against the horrors and damnation preached by his religion and began searching for a more positive societal shaper, eventually settling on education. He believed that a well-designed education system and curriculum could take the lead in bringing order to an increasingly chaotic society as more and more immigrants poured into the country. The legal system could not meet this need because law was aimed mainly at adults whose ideas and values were already set. Education had a better chance because it reached children and helped shape their character.

The dominant belief that religious training in school was necessary to create good, moral citizens remained during this period. Mann argued that a more comprehensive approach was required, but an approach that continued to incorporate the basic moral doctrines of Christianity. He also proposed teaching the fundamental beliefs upon which the nation had been built, such as the importance of the vote as a vehicle for social change as opposed to violence and revolution.

Concerning economics, Mann felt that education could be the key to poor people improving their situation and, thus, narrowing the wealth gap between "capital," or the owners, and "labor," or the workers. His thinking contradicted that of previously mentioned Adam Smith who put his faith in an economic system, laissez faire, as the vehicle that would help the poor close the gap, rather than in education. Of course, in Smith's case, things didn't work out, mainly because the wealthy didn't play by the rules, invalidating the law of supply and demand with strategies such as monopolies and political graft so that eventually the government was forced to step in and to legislate constraints. Education had a better chance of achieving this objective because "capital" had less control, less opportunity to take over the system, to buy it off, to reshape it to satisfy the desires of industrial leaders.

Mann worked tirelessly to integrate Massachusetts's school network, to broaden the curriculum, to extend the number of years students were required to spend in class, to improve the salaries of teachers, and to improve teacher education. His six main principles were (1) that the public should no longer remain ignorant; (2) that such education should be paid for, controlled, and sustained by an interested public; (3) that education would be best provided in schools that embrace children from a variety of backgrounds; (4) that education must be nonsectarian; (5) that education must be taught by the spirit, methods, and discipline of a free society; and (6) that education should be provided by well-trained, professional teachers.

Mann's foundational belief, like Thomas Jefferson's, was that no society could remain free unless the public was educated. After implementing his system in Massachusetts he spent the rest of his career speaking and sharing his ideas with other states (Horace Mann, Wikipedia).

Henry Barnard (1811–1900) led the same sort of crusade in Connecticut. One of his most important contributions was *Barnard's Journal*, a publication read nationally and then internationally that presented data from the realm of education, new ideas and teaching techniques, and comments on recent educational legislation. His journal was the first to tie the education interests of the entire nation together. The last post held by Barnard was that of first U.S. Commissioner of Education where he directed the new Federal Bureau of Education, an organization created to gather and disseminate data nationally.

While public school systems were developing mainly in cities under the guidance of Mann, Barnard, and others to provide primary education, increasing numbers of academies sprang up that carried the formal learning experience into what we would now call a secondary or high school level. As academies received no government funding, their existence depended on them finding or creating markets. Very few, if any, had the resources necessary to branch out to other

locations. The survival of an academy, therefore, was frequently tenuous. As the tax-supported primary public school
system grew, its offerings were expanded vertically to include
the secondary level. Many of the academies that could not
compete were absorbed and converted into high schools, their
teachers being absorbed as well.

4.4 Dealing with the Flood of Immigrants

As the United States moved toward the mid-1800s, its population swelled rapidly. In the beginning of the century the
population was roughly 5,000,000. By 1850, it had reached
23,000,000, more than 1,000,000 Irish alone crossing the
ocean to find opportunity, driven out of their homeland by
the potato famine and by the mercenary practices of absentee
British landlords. By 1860, the U.S. population had reached
roughly 31,500,000 and from there it increased by roughly
1,000,000 each year until 1900 (Spring, 1994, p. 96).

The need for a better-organized education system became
rapidly apparent, the underlying realization being that if the
individuals flooding into the country from different parts of
the world were to contribute to its economic growth they
needed to learn at least the basics. Most importantly, they
needed familiarity with the English language, both written
and spoken. At this point in U.S. history, therefore, the concept of a system of free education for all was transformed
by circumstances from an intellectual ideal to a necessity, if
only as a means of establishing and maintaining order among
the growing masses. Owing to the involved realization, an
integrated network of common schools was established,
partially as a means of assuring dominance of a Protestant,
Anglo-American culture; but also as a way to reduce tensions
between social classes; to eliminate crime and poverty; to
stabilize the political system; and to create patriotic citizens
(Spring, 1994, p. 96).

Trouble materialized immediately. The group having the most difficulty with the emphasis on public schools supporting a Protestant culture was the several million Irish Catholics who had recently immigrated to the United States. The Catholic community complained, seeking to have its views and traditions honored and not attacked in the curriculum. For example, Catholic parents wanted their children to read the Catholic version of the Bible during religious instruction. The involved arguments led to appeals to state governments, to court cases and, eventually, to riots during which people were killed. When little sympathy for the Catholic concerns was generated, the Church took matters into its own hands and built its own system of parish schools, obliging Catholic parents to send their children to them.

Despite the departure of Catholics, the public common school system continued to expand. Communities and the countryside were divided into districts, each required to include at least one primary school. Most of these schools had one room where students of all ages sat and learned together. Individual school districts pretty much controlled the operation of their school. Local inhabitants interviewed and hired teachers, decided when their school would be open, were responsible for maintenance, and levied local taxes to support the school. Since the amount raised was frequently insufficient, an additional tax called a "rate–bill" was levied on families with children attending. Unfortunately, this additional sum sometimes forced poorer families who could not afford it to withdraw their children. Also, wealthier districts could allocate more tax revenues to support their school, putting students in the poorer districts at a disadvantage so that although the organizational reasons for such an arrangement were obvious, it went against the ideal of equal educational opportunity advocated by our founding fathers.

As the number of young people eligible to become students continued to increase markedly across the country, calls for greater integration of school systems—first at the state, then at the national level—grew, along with calls for centralization of policy-making efforts, along with calls for standardization of curriculum. Laws making attendance compulsory at the elementary school level had by this time been passed in most states. Originally, children aged 8–14 were required to attend at least 12 weeks of primary schooling a year. In the late 1800s, Chicago led the way by raising the number of required weeks to 16 and saying that at least eight of them had to be consecutive.

The logic behind this move reflected not only the belief of Thomas Jefferson, Horace Mann, and others that education was necessary to a strong democracy, but also the desire to use the schools as a vehicle to *Americanize* the growing flood of new immigrants and to make them productive. Many were afraid of the country being overrun, its culture diluted or buried or destroyed. Obviously, more instructors were required to handle the rapidly growing number of students. Women teachers soon outnumbered their male counterparts, though the men continued to earn more than twice as much for the same workload.

4.5 Frederick Froebel Gives Us Kindergarten

By this time the public education network in at least the country's largest cities included kindergarten, primary schools, high schools, vocational schools, normal schools for the training of future teachers, and night schools for those who worked during the day. The concept of a "kindergarten," translated as a "children's garden," had been introduced by the German educator, Frederick Froebel (1782–1852) in 1840. He said that teachers "should be passive and protective, not directive and interfering." (Froebel, 1895, pp. 1–15). He taught that rather than programming children to the dictates of society at this early stage in life when they were most malleable and open to learning, they should be placed in an environment that facilitated discovery and unleashing of their natural, individual potential. The principle activity of children attending kindergarten, according to Froebel, should be to "play" because he considered play to be the wellspring of creativity.

Froebel saw children as growing like plants. They needed to be fed a steady diet of intellectually stimulating activities. Thus, he provided balls, spheres, cubes cylinders, building blocks, paper, along with materials for modeling and weaving to encourage the development of motor skills. He also believed that children should be exposed to socializing experiences early in life. To generate such experiences, interaction with other students was encouraged while the provided objects were being played with. The end purpose of Froebel's kindergarten education was to help children begin to understand their personal reality and the interconnectedness of all things.

While Froebel's original German versions of kindergarten focused on stimulating creative play and self-expression, the early U.S. kindergartens focused initially on providing positive socialization for children who grew up in slums, on helping them develop self-awareness and self-esteem, and on instilling a sense of order and discipline. Kindergartens had been introduced previously in the U.S. private school sector. The first public school sector kindergarten was begun in 1873 in a St. Louis tenement neighborhood, to deal with the growing poverty and crime found there. The objective was to gain control over children's lives at an earlier age. The kindergarten was to provide the moral training not provided by the family or the community. It was also used as a vehicle for sending messages home to parents, getting them to focus on greater cleanliness and improved morality.

Summer schools were opened as a means of keeping city children busy so that they did not get into trouble. Playgrounds were added to school complexes for the additional purpose of helping kids develop physically. Lunch programs were put into place to help deal with nutritional shortcomings. Nurses joined the school staff to deal with health issues. Showers were installed so that students could be bathed in an attempt to get rid of the lice and filth carried in from their homes. A movement began to make schools community social centers as well as education centers. Events such as concerts, plays, fairs, political discussions were held there. School lobbies were used for art exhibits and competitions. By the early 1900s, it was found that more than half of all students in U.S. public schools had foreign-born parents. Night classes were put into place to facilitate the "Americanization" process of their parents. The classes offered lessons on things such as the English language, how democracy works, what immigrants needed to do to gain citizenship.

Chapter 5

Education in the United States during the Late 1800s

5.1 A Broadening of Emphasis

In 1896 John Dewey (1859–1952), an educational philosopher, set up the Laboratory School at the University of Chicago in order to conduct studies and experiments in his field. Dewey wanted to bind the home, the community, and the school closely together. He wanted children to be able to use their everyday experiences in the home and in the community to facilitate the learning process at school. He stressed that teaching should be built not around lecture and memorization but around real-life experiences and discussions. In his Laboratory School, he developed models that tied class lessons to community building exercises, thus encouraging students to use their "social imagination" to discover ways to make life better for everyone.

As other philosophers before him, Dewey also believed that children learn best by doing, and that as frequently as possible they should be involved in hands-on learning experiences.

Curriculum should be designed such that while learning practical skills they have shown an interest in—say, carpentry or cooking or weaving—they should also be learning math, reading, and writing, thus making them more well-rounded and better prepared to deal with life. One of the new pieces of this model was the use of museums to teach. Exhibits were set up so that students could learn about different cultures and about different manufacturing processes—for example, the transition of raw cotton into finished fabric.

At the other end of the academic continuum, at the college level, owing to the fact that by 1862 agriculture remained the country's main industry involving more than 90% of the population, President Lincoln signed the *Morrill Act*, making funds available for each state to buy land in order to establish colleges dedicated to agricultural science and to the mechanical arts related to farming. The act and the ensuing movement were extremely popular, and for good reason. The United States has more land that could be farmed productively than any other country in the world. Thomas Jefferson is the one who visualized its main industry as remaining agriculture; its future role as being to help feed the rest of the world. As part of this movement, the collection of agriculture-related data began in earnest so that farming techniques could be improved and yields increased.

As was said before, prior to the Revolutionary War, a total of nine colleges had been established in the colonies mainly to train minister and, to a lesser extent, political leaders. Between the Revolutionary War and the Civil War, a period of approximately 90 years, some 250 more were established, mainly by groups or individuals harboring narrow religious interests (Spring, pp. 69–70). During this latter period, a battle arose between leaders who believed college curriculum should stick to the classics—centering on Latin, Greek, and history—and leaders encouraging a shift of focus to more "useful" subjects such as science and language. Supporters of traditional curriculum believed that the major purpose of a college education is to facilitate the fullest possible development of students' mental faculties, of their ability to reason, and of their ability to learn. Those supporting the more practical curriculum wanted colleges to deliver knowledge that would facilitate the pursuit of improvement in student's economic status.

Another, related debate that gained strength, a continuation of the previously mentioned one that arose following the Revolutionary War, was between those believing that college curriculum should help shape students into good patriots and Christians and those who believed that it should, instead, help cultivate the skills necessary for students to reason out their own values. Institutions that had adopted the shaping philosophy encouraged students to live in campus dormitories so that their daily activities, both in-class and out-of-class, could be supervised. This arrangement was considered necessary as part of the institution's responsibility to help shape moral character as well as intellect.

A third debate that arose concerned how much control the government should be allowed to exercise over private educational institutions chartered by the state. In the Dartmouth College case of 1819, Daniel Webster argued for the college and Chief Justice John Marshall of the Supreme Court wrote the decision. The outcome was that private colleges should be free of such control; that they should be treated like private corporations in this respect; that if states wanted to exercise control over institutions of higher learning they should create their own system.

Then, in 1876, based on the more comprehensive model of German graduation education, the city of Baltimore founded Johns Hopkins University, the first in the United States to offer a PhD. Its graduate program was designed to train future college professors. Clark University in Worcester, Massachusetts was the second to offer a graduate studies program followed by Harvard, Yale, the University of Chicago, what is now Stanford University in California, and a growing number of other institutions.

5.2 The Education Sector Gets a Voice

The National Education Association was formed in 1857 when 43 educators gathered in Philadelphia to develop a united voice for public education. Partially as a result of the Association's efforts, a steady stream of subjects was added to the curriculum so that students were sometimes studying as many as 16 or 17 subjects under the guidance of two or three teachers. Thirty-five years later, in 1892, a government-sponsored group called "The Committee of Ten" on Secondary School Studies was formed to rethink entrance requirements for students interested in going on to college. Up to that point, different colleges and universities required different things, which made it difficult for high schools to put together an appropriate preparatory curriculum.

During the 1800s an increasing number of required testing areas had also been added to the original Latin and Greek college/university entrance exams. The additions included common mathematics, English grammar, geography, algebra, geometry, Greek and Roman history, American history, physical geography, French, and, finally, German. At any point in their educational process, if students could pass the college or university's entrance exam, they were admitted, no matter what their academic background. Students could even begin taking college courses while finishing secondary school requirements, which is interesting in light of the model this book will eventually present.

The major issue that arose during this period was whether or not secondary school courses taken by students headed for college should differ from those designed for students headed directly into the workplace? Or should the focus be on insuring that every student received a good general education across the spectrum of available curriculum? The committee's eventual decision was that all students should have access to all courses. As one of its members stated, "There is no reason why one child should study Latin and another be limited to the 'three Rs'" (Krug, pp. 169–170).

The driving concept in the economic sector during the late 1800s and early 1900s was "social efficiency," which, of course, sprang from the workplace focus on ever-increasing efficiencies of production. As a result, industrialists wanted the education sector to concentrate on the development of each student's "useful" potential. These men wanted students to specialize rather than to generalize, to complete studies in a specific area rather than picking from the full spectrum of courses.

This attitude, of course, did not fit well with the decision of The Committee of Ten so that a compromise had to be reached. Eventually, introductory courses were designed that all high school students would be required to take. Then students would move into one of four tracts of study, including Classical Studies, Latin Scientific heavy on the science end, a Modern Language sequence, and English. There was some crossing over between the tracts. The objective, of course, was to give students access to as many useful areas of study as possible, and not to deny anything to anyone.

Also, the committee recommended that sufficient time be spent on each subject taught to ensure real learning and understanding, a recommendation that eliminated the "scattershot approach" of too many different subjects being taught. Finally, the committee recommended that the students not headed for college but immediately into the workplace receive the same level of rigorous instruction as those headed for college.

Not many schools, however, instituted the Committee of Ten's suggested reforms wholesale. Many objected to the continuing emphasis on foreign languages, especially Latin. Many expressed the need for even more training in the sciences. The Committee's main accomplishment was to set a precedent for future improvement efforts (Noble, p. 316).

Owing to the pressure exerted partly by industrialists, the need to teach cooperation also became apparent. Each individual graduate who moved directly into the workplace needed to be a specialist, good at what he or she did. But the individuals also had to learn to work together. A high school teacher named Collin Scott helped lead an effort to institute what we now call the team approach to learning. Scott would discover common interests among his students, then form groups around those interests, and have members work together on a related project.

5.3 Change Comes Slow

At this point in history, the three concepts around which the high school educational culture was being shaped were equality of opportunity, development of individual potential, and learning to work cooperatively. Obviously, the three did not always compliment each other. Frequently, in fact, they clashed. In 1899, The Committee on College Entrance Requirements was formed to revisit at least one of the issues originally addressed by The Committee of Ten. This committee eventually established a uniform list of required topics and units of work in each high school subject for students wanting to continue onto college. It developed the concept of "core courses," those required, while the rest, eventually called "electives," could be selected by the student. The committee's main objective was to "level the playing field," creating a valid method of comparing student academic credentials (Noble, p. 317).

In the meantime, colleges and universities began developing programs for high school teachers, leaving the training of future common school teachers to the normal schools. In 1889, the first comprehensive teacher's college was established in conjunction with Columbia University. The college provided a liberal arts education. Degrees were earned by gaining the knowledge and technical skills necessary to be an effective teacher. The college helped gain credibility for the profession, awarding masters degrees, then, eventually, PhDs.

By the late 1800s, the bureaucratic form of administration had been introduced throughout the public education sector in an attempt to bring order to all levels and to help clearly define the responsibilities of staff as well as students. A hierarchy of superintendents beginning at the state level and reaching down through the counties to the local level was established and given a growing range of responsibilities and authority. For each school, a board of directors elected from the community now oversaw educational efforts rather than the local government or the community at large. Individual schools were under the direction of a principal to whom the teachers reported.

The orderliness of the hierarchical arrangement was supposed to provide a model for students, helping them prepare for the demands of the industrial workplace. Teachers placed strong emphasis on things such as maintaining a good attendance record, arriving to class on time, and having their work completed. The first school where students were separated by age into grades was the Quincy Common School in Massachusetts opened in 1848. Each classroom held up to 56 students of one age rather than a much greater number of mixed ages. The single-room schoolhouse, however, the rural schoolhouse attended by all students, persisted until the early 1900s (Spring, p. 141).

The overall development of the public school system remained slow, a majority of young people opting, usually out of necessity, for work rather than education. High school attendance, unlike grade school attendance, was not required by law. By 1880, only one young person among 50 continued onto the secondary level. By 1920, this number had improved from one to five. Many of those who did enroll, however, dropped out before graduation (Button, p. 125). It was widely agreed that the purpose of education prior to the mid-1800s was mainly to develop in students "memory, will, and judgment" through study of the classics and mathematics. Following that point in time, owing to the Industrial Revolution in large part, a new goal was added—the absorption of large quantities of information from an expanding range of more practical subjects.

The fields of law, engineering, physics, botany, geology, etc. were becoming increasingly important as a support to the nation's escalating obsession with growth. Business schools also began to spring up with the financial backing of industrialists. Their role was to train specialists—mainly accountants, bookkeepers, and those skilled in finance. The training gained at these schools was delivered at the high school level, as was that offered by the new manual arts schools teaching skills needed on the factory floor—wood and metal working, machine maintenance and repair, machine and building construction.

It must be remembered, however, that while the Industrial Revolution was getting started, a majority of U.S. citizens were still farmers. Although land-grant colleges had been established to serve this population, finding students willing and able to attend was an ongoing problem. Farmers showed little interest in formal education, especially higher-level formal education. In response, the Federal Government in 1889 established a number of agricultural high schools throughout the country. The main subjects taught were in the field of agriculture or were oriented toward agriculture as a means of preparing students for college, though more traditional subjects were included. The idea of separating the involved students from more general high school curriculum, however, proved unacceptable and the agricultural schools were eventually folded into the mainstream, though, as a compromise, agriculture was added to the required list of subjects that public schools offered.

During this period, *William McGuffey's Readers* (1800–1873) replaced the original *New England Primer* as the most popular texts for instruction in reading along with a smattering of other subjects. McGuffy's publications included a primer, a speller, and four readers, others being added in later years. They were instrumental in setting the societal tone of the day. The McGuffey readers included stories for young children, more advanced writings by a range of authors for older students, historical and religious offerings, and poetry. The focus was on building moral character and on encouraging students to accept and make the best of their lot in life. Reverting to Calvinism, the inference was that the possession of great wealth was equivalent to the achievement of salvation. Those so blessed, however, were expected in return to love and help the poor who, in return, were expected to not resent the wealthy but to be grateful that the wealthy were concerned about their situation. The *Readers*, obviously, were designed to help reinforce the *status quo* in terms of social class and the growing gap between the rich and the poor.

Chapter 6

Influences during the Industrial Revolution

6.1 The Industrial Revolution Reshapes the U.S. Education System

The U.S. version of the Industrial Revolution picked up steam following the Civil War (1860–1865) and greatly affected the nation's educational culture. It was driven by laissez faire economic thinking and by the country's desire to catch up with Europe and become a major player on the world's economic stage. By 1875, the French Commissioner of Education, after touring schools throughout the country, wrote that education had become an essential part of the U.S. system of governance, and that schools trained student to be patriots, be they from established families or from the families of newly arrived immigrants. He also said that the curriculum in U.S. schools focused on providing applicable workplace skills that would contribute to the country's economic growth.

As the Industrial Revolution progressed, the humanities increasingly lost their appeal. Emphasis was on teaching "the science of high production." This attitude sifting quickly down from the college and university level to the secondary and even to the primary school levels. Art education, for example, was no longer viewed as an opportunity to awaken the sensitivities, and to expand the perception of students. Rather, it served mainly as a way to produce skilled draftsmen for the industrial sector.

Another major change was that training in technical skills was now received from hands-on experience in a classroom/school workshop setting rather than from the traditional apprenticeship system. Obviously, more craftsmen could be produced this way in less time; they could be "mass produced," mirroring the societal emphasis on the increasingly efficient mass-production of consumer goods and services.

There was, of course, negative reaction to this "mechanistic" approach to education. The line in the sand was drawn quickly between the two competing schools of thought. Those who advocated the mechanistic approach and those who advocated educating students to resemble machine parts, shaping them so that they fit neatly into the production process, were represented by the "Robber Barons," a group of some 20 men and one woman who gained control of the U.S. economy following the Civil War and held sway into the early 1900s.

We all know the names of some of these people—J.P. Morgan, who dominated the banking industry; Andrew Carnegie, best known for his activities in the steel industry; John D. Rockefeller, the oil magnate; Jay Gould, Jay Cooke, Cornelius Vanderbilt. The U.S. economic philosophy at that point was as close as it has ever been to pure laissez faire—the greatest good will come to the greatest number if every person pursues his or her own self-interest, if every person strives to gain as much personal wealth as possible with no concern for the well-being of others while the government stays out of it, does not try to regulate what is going on.

Once the wealth was accumulated by the most driven, the most talented, the theory was that it would "trickle down."

Instead of hoarding it, or using it to outdo each other in terms of the impression pieces gathered, the wealthy would use it to create new industry and new jobs. This actually did happen to a certain extent. The country's infrastructure was built in large part through efforts of the Robber Barons. But it did not happen to the extent necessary to keep the society healthy. Unemployment frequently hovered around 30% during the reign of these men. The country suffered a depression or a severe recession approximately every 10 years.

As laissez faire advocates, the Robber Barons were obsessed with winning, with making as much money as possible, then using that money to make even more. J.P. Morgan, at one point, was asked by a reporter if "some statement were not due the public" after the machinations of his banking empire had caused a panic and great loss to investors. True to character, his reply was, "I owe the public nothing."

The Robber Barons pretty much owned the U.S. government during their reign, feeling no qualms about buying politicians and their votes when it was advantageous, sometimes bragging publicly about doing so. They also understood the value of the education system to their future, funding the startup of a number of upper-level institutions, including Carnegie Mellon, (Andrew Carnegie), Vanderbilt University (Cornelius Vanderbilt), Spelman University (John D. Rockefeller), and Duke University (James Buchanan Duke), with the curriculum offered by these institutions designed, in large part, to produce technicians.

6.2 Frederick Taylor's Scientific Management Spills Over into the Classroom

The person whose contribution did the most to shape the mechanistic school of thought and bring it to life was a Philadelphian named Frederick Taylor (1856–1915). Taylor was a self-trained mechanical engineer who turned down a Harvard education to go to work in a factory and learn what he was interested in learning hands-on. He dedicated his career to discovering ways to improve efficiencies in the workplace. He believed that there were two major problems in the industrial sector. First, concerning technology, there was a lack of standardization. Second, concerning management processes, there was also a lack of standardization.

His objective in terms of the latter was to design work so that employees were required to think as little as possible and to make no production-related decisions. His aim was to find ways to program employees to operate in the most efficient manner and to reward them for doing so. The approach Taylor fathered in order to achieve this objective was labeled "Scientific Management." He applied the principles of scientific analysis to his improvement efforts.

Taylor's best-known experiment took place at the Bethlehem Steel Company in Bethlehem, Pennsylvania. He began by dividing jobs into the simplest, possible elementary movements and discarding the ones he found useless. He then studied the motions of individual workers using a stopwatch to discover the quickest method of completing the involved task. Also, he studied other time-consuming activities such as work breaks, getting warmed up in the morning, interacting with other employees, and sought ways to shape these activities so that they took less time without negatively affecting productivity. His overall philosophy regarding work and production could be summed up as

1. Break the work process into the smallest possible components.
2. Fit jobs into structures that clearly emphasize the duties and boundaries of each individual job rather than its part in the total process.

3. Whenever possible, use individual or small group monetary incentives, tying pay to output.
4. Subtract skill and responsibility from the job and make them functions of management (Sass, pp. 19–20).

Managers were not expected to think either. Every morning they reported to a "planning room" where that day's production requirement and related activities would be mapped out for them. The managers were not called on to contribute to this process all decisions having been made before they arrived. Their job was to deliver hand-written instructions to workers describing what was expected, the time that should be spent accomplishing each task, and the step-by-step procedures to be followed. Managers were then required to oversee and guide the employees' efforts.

Three additional responsibilities were added. The first was to keep records and gather the data necessary for the scientific redesign and improvement of the work overseen. The second was to select and train workers. The third was to ensure that employees under their control completed tasks the way they had been trained to complete them, following the principles of scientific management.

The workplace culture created by Taylor and other social scientists during this period obviously impacted educational philosophy. The purpose of schooling according to these people was to generate graduates who could contribute to the free enterprise economy, at least 75% of which, at that point, was primary industry. Emphasis was on teaching students to do what they were told to do, to learn what they were told to learn, with "unquestioning obedience" (Sound familiar?). Discussion was not encouraged. Students simply listened, wrote down what they heard, and regurgitated it for tests. What students were required to learn at each level was clearly spelled out. None of this "doing your own thing" stuff was encouraged because it wasted time.

6.3 Opposition Arises to the Mechanistic Approach

On the other side of that line drawn in the sand, resided people who found serious fault with the "mechanistic" approach in both the workplace and the education sector. Concerning the workplace, Samuel Gompers, then president of the AFL, wrote,

> "So there you are wage-workers in general, mere machines – considered industrial, of course. Hence, why should you not be standardized and your motion-power brought up to the highest possible perfection in all respects, including speeds? Not only your length, breadth, and thickness as a machine, but your grade of hardness, malleability, tractability, and general serviceability, can be ascertained, regis-tered, and then employed as desired by your owners. Science would thus get the most out of you before you are sent to the junkpile" (Sudhir, p. 183).

Social scientists on the "anti-mechanistic" side of the line formed the "human relations" school of thought. Their ranks included Mary Follet, who argued that employees were more productive when treated like human beings rather than machines. She said that workers had the same needs during working hours as they had in their lives outside work, and that productivity increased when these needs were taken into account and efforts made to meet them. She said that decision-making should be more participative, that being asked to con-tribute provided workers with a valuable learning experience and encouraged commitment.

Elton Mayo and Fritz Rothlisberger, two Harvard professors, made a serious contribution to the human relations side of the argument during research at the Western Electric Company

Hawthorne Plant near Chicago. Their assignment was to measure the effect of improved lighting on productivity in a workshop. Eventually, they showed that, yes, the improved lighting did increase productivity. But, more importantly, they showed that because they had sought input from workers during the experiment, allowed workers to participate, and that because they had taken the workers' ideas and needs into account, productivity increased even more so. The results of their project helped proved Follet's theory to be correct, that employees are more productive when asked to become involved in the problem-solving and decision-making processes.

Unions protested strongly against the introduction of manual training into the public school curriculum as a means of mass-producing future line workers and factory managers. Unions said that shifting it to the education sector would flood the market with poorly trained craftsmen. They were especially against introducing manual training at the elementary school level where it would replace the more traditional subjects required for students to function effectively in normal society. William Torrey Harris (1835–1909), superintendent of St. Louis public schools during this period and a widely respected academician, joined the unions in voicing strong opposition to the introduction of manual training as a major part of public school education. He said that the system should stick to teaching grammar, literature, mathematics, geography, and history, which he described as "the five windows of the soul" critical to understanding ourselves, our society, and nature. He saw the manual training movement as focusing on physical development to the exclusion of spiritual development.

Advocates of manual training in the lower levels of the public school system countered by saying that childhood, indeed, was the ideal time. Children were still malleable and could more easily be taught such skills, could more easily be programmed. Such advocates had the industrial wealth of the nation on their side so that as the Industrial Revolution progressed, the introduction of manual training into the public school curriculum gained increasing amounts of support. Families of public school students during this period were, as we have said, usually poor. They, as well, wanted their children to learn income-producing skills as soon as possible and joined with the wealthy in calling for it.

6.4 Rationalizations for Educating Students to Be Robots

As a result of the design of increasingly sophisticated technology and the growing emphasis on mass production the range of skills required by workers was progressively being narrowed. Unlike the era of guild membership that flourished during the Medieval Period and on through the Renaissance and Reformation, craftsmen no longer produced an entire, finished pair of shoes or wheel-borrow or chair. Rather, as a result of the "division of labor" they were being trained to contribute only a part of each product—according to Frederick Taylor the smallest possible part—so that no thinking and little or no skill was required. This approach enabled children to hold full-time jobs in that their responsibilities were usually limited to repeating the same motion over and over and over and over for the entire day, week, and month. The mission of owners (many said "the God-given mission") was again to get as much productivity as possible out of their employees for a little reward as possible. Pay for such a job has been recorded to be as low as 42 cents for a 14 hours a day, six days a week. This breaks down to three cents an hour and didn't help much to improve the child's situation (Button, p. 164).

Youngsters who were able to find employment obviously didn't have time for much else in their lives. By the early 1900s, laws in most states required children to attend both grade school and high school, but factory owners simply ignored the laws and kept no records concerning the hours spent by children at their machines. Public schools in poor urban neighborhoods frequently did not keep attendance records either so that children who couldn't find work often roamed the streets, doing whatever it took to bring home a few pennies. In a strange twist of fate, the manufactory owners, realizing the threat such street urchins posed to their security, began supporting compulsory public school education as a means of keeping them under control.

Between 1890 and 1914, more than 1.5 million more immigrants flooded into the United States, mostly into major east coast cities. At that point in history, the U.S. government provided no welfare safety net it included no department with a charge similar to that of today's Department of Health and Human Services. Part of the cultural reasoning behind this shortcoming was the popular role model of the "self-made man" strongly encouraged by the Robber Barons and their admirers. The belief was that people willing to accept help from others were showing weakness and laziness. They were showing the lack of the drive that was the cornerstone of the fledgling U.S. economy. In order to stop such people from becoming a drain on society, and in order to thwart their efforts to prevent others from gaining well-earned rewards through hard work, no such support should be offered.

Herbert Spenser of Great Britain (1820–1903), with assistance from William Graham Sumner (1840–1910), a Yale professor, developed a popular rationalization, eventually called "Social Darwinism," for the inhumane treatment and exploitation of employees. Theirs was the latest in a steady stream of historical rationalizations for such attitudes. Long before Spenser and Sumner came Niccolo Machiavelli (1469–1527). During the Renaissance Period, Machiavelli offered, mainly through his writings, the concept of "Machiavellian Humanism." The Greek concept of "Humanism," made popular by thinkers during that period, centered on the human aspects of life, on making life better for individual humans and for society as a whole, learning how to do so through studying the works of the ancients.

Machiavelli twisted humanist teachings into, "do whatever it takes to improve your personal situation with no concern for the cost to others and to society as a whole." The core value he espoused was "every man for himself," saying at one point that is it better and more profitable for leaders "to be feared than loved" when using the efforts of others as a vehicle for self-improvement.

Next came Adam Smith (1723–1790), considered the father of laissez faire economic theory. A social philosopher, Smith was disturbed by the effects of regulation and taxes on economic growth. As an Enlightenment Period thinker he believed, like many of the other great minds busy reshaping European and, to a lesser extent, U.S. society, that because the physical laws governing the universe had been discovered by Sir Isaac Newton, its workings should be understandable. Therefore, every system contained within that universe should be understandable as well. All one had to do was discover the governing law or laws.

Smith's search was in the realm of economics. The governing law he discovered was "the law of supply and demand." He wrote in his book, *An Inquiry into the Nature and Causes of the Wealth of Nations,* that if government left the economic sector alone, did not try to regulate it, the sector would self-regulate through the natural law of supply and demand—that is, of course, if everybody played by the rules. When asked what was to prevent the more ambitious from breaking the rules, for example, from forming monopolies or cartels in order to eliminate competition and control pricing, Smith's response was, "Man's inner good," that those running the factories and mills would understand the value to themselves and to society in general of sharing the wealth generated, especially with their employees.

Smith's faith in his fellow man was, of course, rapidly betrayed. The problem was that he did not understand the previously mentioned scarcity mentality, and its effect on people. Eventually Smith became disillusioned with what his ideas had wrought and began calling for increased government regulation. But it was too late. Laissez faire economic theory had become the cornerstone of economic progress.

Sir Thomas Malthus (1766–1834), discussed in Chapter 2, provided a third serious rationalization for exploitation of the poor that made him extremely popular with early industrialists eager to find acceptable excuses for their excesses. And finally came the rationalization we started with, Spencer's and Sumner's Social Darwinism. Charles Darwin (1809–1882), another brilliant thinker and doer, gave us the *Theory of Evolution*. Darwin believed and began the process of proving that rather than being placed on the Earth "as is" by God, man as we now know him evolved through millions of years from a more primitive being, as did all species. One of the things that made this evolution successful was "survival of the fittest." The fittest members of the species, those with characteristics that allowed them to deal most effectively with the environment and environmental change, were the ones who survived and procreated, passing their adaptability onto the next generation.

Spenser and Sumner prostituted Darwin's work, proclaiming that the modern day workplace should be treated as an evolutionary process, that the strong (owners) should be encouraged to dominate, should be allowed to feed off of the relatively weak (workers) in any way they saw fit, that this approach benefited society, that if the needs of the weak were considered and catered to, society would suffer. This attitude, of course, reverts back to Machiavellian Humanism's "every man for himself" and was supported by no scientific evidence at all.

6.5 The Battle between Mechanists and Humanists

Lester Frank Ward (1841–1913), who has been described as the father of American sociology, opposed Spenser and Sumner, arguing that rather than giving into the natural, uncontrollable human instinct to compete and dominate, rather than believing that nature and the evolutionary process shape our behavior and that we can do nothing about it, man is capable of overcoming what Ward called "natural tendencies" and has the ability to shape his behavior, molding it to benefit others as well as himself and to benefit society as a whole.

While this argument raged, inner cities continued to decay owing to the lack of tax-generated funds, the collection of which was obviously opposed by survival of the fittest fans, and owing to the desire of industrialists to keep employees poor and dependent so that they could more easily be controlled. The public school system serving those neighborhoods lacked the financing necessary to meet the needs of mainly immigrant students.

In reaction to this shortcoming, private citizens started the Progressive Movement, the main purpose of which was to eliminate corruption in the government and industrial sectors and to modernize society. One of the things those in the movement did was to borrow the concept of "social settlement houses" from England and to begin establishing such houses in major U.S. cities. Well-educated young men and women, while attending college and during the years that followed, worked and sometimes lived in social settlement houses dealing directly with the issues of the poor, pulling kids out of the street, teaching them as well as their parents to read and speak English, organizing the kids into sports teams and choirs, tending to their physical ailments.

During the early 1800s, two other important movements also began. While our founding fathers had advocated the establishment of free public libraries, while some 29 had been opened in the colonies, the movement did not really take off until 1820 when the first "legitimate" public library, The Boston Apprentice's Library, was established. After that, the desire for what was offered spread rapidly, libraries being built in large and small communities so that by 1876 when The

American Library Association was formed, there were over 3000 such institutions spread across the states.

The second movement was the creation of lyceums. The first lyceum was established also in Massachusetts in 1826. The purpose of these informal organizations was to offer to the public lectures by learned individuals and to provide a forum for the discussion of ideas and concepts, of new advances in science, of world events.

At this same time, however, the towers of education continued to be assaulted by industrialists who remained obdurate in their demand that the process be shaped to meet their needs. The mechanistic mentality continued to dominate. While adults in lyceums discussed and debated freely, students in the public school system learned mainly through rote memorization and the parroting of answers. In some schools, they had to sit stiffly in the chairs and were not allowed to move any part of their bodies while being instructed, eyes fastened on the teacher. The fact that they might have a thought of their own, an opinion or a probing question was not a consideration. That was not what they were in school for.

Chapter 7

Education in the United States during the Early 1900s

7.1 Psychologists Get Involved in Shaping Education Policy

During the early 1900s, another extremely important voice joined the education debate. That voice belonged to people studying and teaching in the relatively new field of psychology, especially child psychology. While before this time individuals including Aristotle, Comenius, Rousseau, Pestalozzi, Jefferson, Froebel, Mann, Barnard, and Harris had addressed some of the involved issues, coming up with models or, more often, parts of models that could be implemented as a means of achieving the desired ends, never before had these studies been formalized. Psychologists using research methodology generated hypotheses and theories, then integrated their findings to better understand child development, the best way to motivate children, the best way to discover and unleash the potential of the individual child.

Edward Thorndike (1874–1949), considered by many as the father of educational psychology, was taught by William James (1842–1910), who believed that learning is passed on initially through a "stimulus–response interaction." If the same response occurred to the same stimulus enough times, it became a habit. This outcome could be sped up by rewarding the desired response when it occurred. James believed that properly shaped habits are important to the maintenance of social order and that a stimulus–response approach should be used in the education systems to shape such habits.

Another important piece of research carried out during this period was that of Ivan Pavlov (1849–1936), a Russian physiologist who showed that the stimulous-response relationship was strengthened if the stimulus itself was viewed by the recipient as a reward and weakened if the stimulus was viewed as a punishment. Such work proved that behavior was not set at birth, as John Calvin had claimed so long ago, but that it could be shaped through education.

Thorndike carried this line of reasoning further, relating it more closely to education. He said that repetition of the "stimulus–response sequence coupled with rewarding the desired response" process was the key to learning. He also said that the testing and measurement of outcomes was critical to understanding how quickly the student was advancing and what level of contribution that student was capable of making.

William Bagley, one of Thorndike's peers, wrote a very popular book entitled *Classroom Management* saying that the key to successful teaching was to reduce the education process to rigid routine based on stimulus–response learning and the development of habits. Students should march to and from class in lockstep, organize their educational materials in a predefined manner, approach and use the same spot on the blackboard every time, that they should remain rigidly attentive and focused on doing things in the most efficient manner.

Of course, this was still the era of Scientific Management in the industrial sector. So the battle between the mechanist school (Thorndike and Bagley) and the humanist school (Dewey and Scott) had spread to the classroom, both sides, again, providing something of value. In large, crowded classes where cultures were mixed, maintaining order was a major concern so that students could learn as much as possible. In smaller classes, more emphasis could be placed on individual development, hands-on experiences, and group activities.

7.2 Three Different Mindsets

It appears that during this period three major mindsets existed concerning what the public education system should provide. The industrialists wanted to produce hard-working employees who learned fast, took orders well, and did not complain. The parents of students wanted their children to be educated well enough to find jobs but also for the involved education to provide an opportunity for upward economic mobility. Teachers wanted education to be a force in remedying the societal breakdown created in large part by the new industrial culture and by the influx of immigrants that overwhelmed public services.

The U.S. education system spent the next century working toward a compromise that would meet the needs of all three groups. During this period, however, a workplace change occurred that greatly affected the education sector. Up until then a majority of children were expected to help in supporting their families by beginning to work before they reached puberty. The employment they held was largely unskilled, like picking "breakers," or rocks, from the coal coming out of mines, or delivering messages, or working in farm fields. With the rapid advances now being made in technology, these jobs began to disappear. Messenger boys, for example, were made unnecessary by the 1876 invention of the telephone.

Not surprisingly, as the need for child laborers was reduced by technology, laws requiring education for the young, that up to then had been largely ignored, were more strenuously enforced. The psychologists encouraged this shift by defining childhood and adolescence as critical developmental periods. If children were not allowed to develop their potential during these years and were forced to spend their time at repetitious, deadening work instead, that potential would be lost.

Also, people such as Lewis Hines (1874–1940) began documenting the plight of children working in textile mills, coal mines, canning factories, plantation fields all over the country, presenting the vacant eyed stare of those who had know nothing but the machines they served for most of their young lives, presenting images that could not be ignored, so that the public outcry grew. Gradually, the Robber Baron crowd, especially those who saw the very young mainly as an expendable vehicle for increasing their own wealth, began losing clout. More people were now voting, with women gaining that right in 1920. Unions that had been formed in the late 1800s began demonstrating real power and focusing on social issues. Soon states started passing laws baring industrialists from hiring employees 13 years of age or younger. Other new laws limited the number of hours young employees were allowed to work each day to eight.

The factory workers and the farmers instead of being championed by educated upper-class advocates took up their own cause and began demanding free education for their children as a right of citizenship. Organized labor, the farmers alliance, the "Popularist Movement" began fighting, sometimes physically, for tougher child labor laws, for laws that required the young to attend school, for better access to schools.

7.3 Mechanistic Thinking Remains Dominant

However, mechanistic thinking would not go away. Frederick Taylor's theories and techniques remained gospel. Consultants became an important part of the industrial scene functioning mainly as efficiency experts, mimicking Taylor and Frank Gilbreth who focused on the motion part of "time–motion studies" using a motion picture camera as a means of recording, analyzing and streamlining individual jobs.

One of the reasons mechanistic thinking did not go away is that the numbers used to measure efficiencies provided a much clearer picture of what was going on in the factory, a picture easier to work with than one including non-quantifiable factors. A second reason was that emphasis remained on generating profit and on finding ways to increase profits by getting the most out of both technical systems and management systems. Again, the desired efficiencies were defined solely in terms of numbers so that employees became part of those numbers, losing their humanness, their needs and wants, and disappearing onto the charts of the consultants and bosses making the decisions.

In the education sector, this same mechanistic approach remained dominant. The research that was being carried out at that point focused on discovering, for example, the most efficient way to teach mathematics? How many students, ideally, should be included in a class? How many minutes should each class period last? How much should be taught in one sitting? Those especially addicted to the numbers went even so far as to calculate the cost per student of learning each subject and to include these calculations in the shaping of curriculum.

Education systems were now obviously being equated to manufacturing processes. Emphasis was on increasing efficiency at all levels. In mathematics classes, for example, how many problems a student could complete correctly in the smallest possible amount of time was what counted. In terms of administration, school districts were consolidated to increase benefits of scale, these benefits being measured by statistical surveys. The concept of "institutionalism" came into good currency. It meant that an education system should be centralized and well organized, that it should focus on standardization, and that it should be driven by utilitarianism—the desire to provide the greatest good for the greatest number.

7.4 Introducing the Concept of Tracts

In terms of high schools, by 1930, 47% of the nation's youth between the ages of 14 and 17 attended, and that percentage increased rapidly as the years passed. Sports, choral groups, acting clubs, debating teams, school newspapers, student government, and all extracurricular activities became part of the offerings as an effort to build positive character, to build a sense of cohesiveness that integrated the diverse ethnic groups and to build a sense of community. The school newspaper and the sporting teams were probably most important in this respect; the newspapers tying people together with information, the sports teams giving all students something common to root for. Student government, which housed elected representatives from all the grades, also gave students a hands-on taste of how democracy functions (Spring, p. 221).

The growing emphasis on providing the greatest good for the greatest number was responsible for an effort to separate students into different tracts based on their potential. The practice was eventually called "streaming" and again originated in Europe. In Germany, for instance, students were assigned to high schools that emphasized different skill sets based on their academic record over the last four years of primary school. In the United States during the early 1900s, school districts began administering a standard test at the end of primary education. According to the score earned on this test students were assigned to a tract beginning in junior high school.

The three possible tracts that eventually evolved over the years were the "honors tract" for college-bound students earning upper-level scores; the "college prep tract" for students who also wanted to attend college but did not score high enough on the test to get into the honors tract; and the "business and vocational tract" where students were required to take the basic courses in traditional subjects, but not the advanced ones. Students on the business side of this third tract learned skills useful in the workplace such as typing, bookkeeping, and short-hand. Students on the vocational side spent time learning skills that might include welding, or automobile mechanics, or, later, working with computer systems.

Initially, an effort was made to have these three sets of students study in different locations, as had been done in Germany, so that they would not interfere with each other's learning and that everybody in one location "spoke the same language." The desire of those making decisions was mainly to separate students in the business and vocational tract from students in the honors and college prep tracts. The Germany school system had done just that and was turning out well-trained factory and office workers who wasted little time on subjects not related directly to their trade.

Undeniably, benefits did come from the mechanistic approach, especially in terms of standardization. But, at the same time, the development of individual potential suffered. Students were being taught in the most efficient manner what they needed to know in order to fit into and contribute to an efficiency-oriented industrial society, one in which, as Taylor recommended, laborers did what they were told to do without question, where increased efficiencies and increased profits were considered inseparable, as two sides of the same coin.

This movement, of course, brought up the question of how to define "the greatest good for the greatest number." Those in the "progressive idealism" camp that traced its roots back to Comenius, Rousseau, and Pestalozzi disagreed strongly with the mechanist's answer. A recent spokesman for the progressive idealism camp was Jean Piaget (1896–1980), a Swiss developmental psychologist and philosopher, who encouraged a child-centered approach to education, believing that education's main purpose should be to release creativity. He said that creativity came from putting textbooks and tests aside, involving students in hands-on experiences, and allowing them to teach themselves instead of turning them into little command-motivated robots.

However, the voices of the industrialists continued to grow stronger as the amount of wealth they generated and controlled increased. As a result, the Smith–Hughes Act was passed by Congress in 1917 expanding the amount of vocational education delivered. The passage of the act was based on the argument that though vocational education excluded many of the classical subjects, it was just as effective as the traditional approach in preparing students to make an adequate living and to contribute.

7.5 Slowly But Surely, Efforts to Educate the Nation Progress

Despite lots of disagreements and lots of battles, or, perhaps, as a result of them, efforts to provide universal, comprehensive education continued to grow stronger. This was demonstrated by the fact that in 1800, an average citizen gained only 82 days of schooling during his or her lifetime while in 1850 that citizen gained 321 days and in 1900 998 days, or approximately five years (Brown, pp. 259–260). In 1880, the yearly school term averaged six-and-a-half months with students attending less than two-thirds of the time. By 1950, that number had reached 9 months with average daily attendance at 88.7% of the student population (Noble, p. 392).

The concept of junior high school also evolved at this point. This new level included seventh, eighth, and ninth grades. During these years, students learned social skills while being introduced to the subject areas they would choose from. The U.S. public education system now had three levels— grades school, junior high school, and high school. During grade school, students were assigned by age-level into class sections where they learned the basics necessary to all areas of study, emphasis being placed on reading, writing, arithmetic, geography, and history. Each section was led by a teacher who presented all academic subjects in the same classroom. Grade school students spent approximately 6 hours a day at school, eating lunch there, and playing outside during recess.

During their three years of junior high school, students transitioned to the young adult world and learned what it had to offer in terms of education. One of the most useful things historically to come out of the period's prevailing efficiency-improving mindset was introduction of the Gary Plan. Classes of students began changing rooms for different subjects, thus creating efficiencies in terms of space usages, which, in turn, saved money. Students remained in the same grade-level sections but moved as a whole from classroom to classroom, from teacher to teacher, from English to algebra to history to language to science to gym to music to art. The involved class break also benefited students, giving them time to collect their thoughts and to "change channels." The grade-level sections were usually small, including perhaps 20 or 30 students. Each was assigned a "homeroom teacher" with whom it met at the beginning of the day so that the teacher could take role, deliver announcements, and listen to problems. Although simply a rearranging of the pieces, the Gary Plan provided such obvious benefits to the education system that it is still in place today.

During their three years of high school or vocational school, students focused on one or several areas of education they might want to pursue in college or the workplace, continuing to move from class to class following homeroom, frequently sitting with different people in different classes. Both junior high school and high school students spent up to eight hours a day at school attending subject sessions and, after regular class hours ended, participating in extracurricular activities such as sports or working on the school newspaper or rehearsing for a play or band practice.

The school board's power to make decisions concerning the running of the school and the shaping of its curriculum diminished during this period while that of school administrators grew. This was due to the growing emphasis on creating a meritocracy in the education sector. While school board members were often rich and powerful members of the community, open to political influence, school administrators had to earn their positions by gaining the required education. While school boards helped define policy, administrators were solely in charge of putting that policy into effect, taking responsibility for record keeping, schedule arrangement, curriculum modification, grading systems, resource planning, and defining student as well as teacher performance.

In 1913, a "small school board bill" was passed that reduced the size of boards from 30 or 40 members—a hang-over from colonial times when the entire community participated—to seven. The bill also said that the election of board members should be city or town-wide rather than by district or neighborhood. This change obviously gave those enjoying the most visibility—community leaders, businessmen, etc.—an advantage. Also, because of the expanded range of voters to which candidates now needed to present and explain their credentials, campaigns became more expensive, giving another advantage to the "elite." Finally, the small school board bill said that the involved elections had to be nonpartisan, which kept political parties from contributing to or otherwise assisting in campaigns. Again, this law gave the wealthy an advantage.

At this point, in the early 1900s, a final player was added to the education sector team. In 1901, Joliet Junior College in Illinois became the first institution of its kind to offer two years of advanced education rather than the four offered by traditional colleges and universities. A distinction was eventually made between junior colleges that were private and leaned toward liberal arts educations and community colleges that were publically funded and tended toward more technical or "useable" degrees.

The two types of institutions played several roles in the education spectrum. First and foremost, students could gain a skill and credentials that would allow them to enter the workforce directly. Second, the community colleges, at least, were cheaper than traditional colleges or universities. Students could complete their general course requirements there, earning an associate's degree, then transfer credits to a traditional college or university to complete courses in their major for a BS or BA degree, saving money in the process. Third, students could take courses in a junior or community college to improve poor grades from high school. Fourth, community members could take courses there for fun or to begin a new career. Fifth, community colleges especially could provide training for the staff of local companies. And finally, outstanding high school students could take advanced courses there that would improve their chances of gaining entrance to a top-tier four-year college or university.

7.6 The Hierarchy in Place: Efforts Shift to Shaping Curriculum

By the early 1900s, therefore, the education hierarchy of the United States was complete, with the role of each level being well defined. Attention now turned to one of the questions that had not gone away. "Where should the academic emphasis be in terms of generating the greatest good for society as a whole?" Conservative thinkers believed that education should be about culture and about intellectual discipline. Only one course of study should be mapped out; all students should be mandated to follow it. Liberal thinkers, on the other hand, believed that a "wise differentiation" should be allowed. Students, after conferring with parents and teachers, should be allowed to pick their own courses.

The compromise reached, at least at the college level, that still stands today, is that students should be allowed to pick their own concentration, but that in each concentration they are required to take certain number of predefined core courses along with the electives they select. The classics-based concentrations came to be called "liberal arts." They included English, philosophy, languages, and history—areas where quantitative measurement of progress and success was sometimes more difficult to achieve, where subjective measurement was frequently required. The practical concentrations included engineering, chemistry, mathematics, and physics—areas where measurement could be totally objective. Increasing numbers of students chose the latter. Study of the original classics continued to fade. In 1900, over 50% of high school students studied Latin. By 1960, that percentage had shrunk to less that 10%. Greek, by this time, had disappeared entirely from the traditional curriculum (Noble, p. 463).

By the early 1900s, an attempt was being made at the public high school level to include as many subjects as possible in order to better prepare students to make the right choices in college or the workplace. A smattering of the classics, say a year of Latin, world history, U.S. history, and/or U.S. literature was to be offered, along with an increasing number of courses important to current economic development—chemistry, mathematics, physics, biology, geography—along with courses to prepare students for jobs in the business world, including typing, accounting, shorthand, drafting, bookkeeping; along with at least one required course in the manual arts or home economics; along with courses in the arts—painting, theater, writing, ceramics singing, learning to play an instrument; and along with athletics including gym class and team sports.

The problem with this arrangement turned out to be that while students were gaining a broad overview of what was out there, they were achieving very little depth of understanding in any one subject area. Also, owing to the superficiality of this approach, emphasis remained too frequently on memorization rather than on improving one's ability to reason effectively, to think creatively (Noble, p. 465). In order to cut down on the number of courses and to enrich those that remained, attempts were eventually made to combine or to "fuse" some of those with complementary content. For example, botany and zoology were "fused" into biology.

Chapter 8

Chapter 8

Education in the United States to the Mid-1900s

8.1 Tumultuous Shifts in the Education System

As a brief summary concerning what transpired in the U.S. academic sector up to this point in history, a gradual but radical shift had occurred in the motivation driving it: this shift moving from a focus on religious training during colonial days to cultural training during the early days of the nation to discipline during the mid and late 1800s to utility during the early 1900s. It had moved from making students good Christians and good citizens toward encouraging students to gain the knowledge and skills required to contribute to economic progress.

Concerning the logistics of the system, until 1920, the major focus had been on getting it into place and on developing the necessary structure and policies at the national, state, county, and local levels. The United States had been in a state of continuous flux since the Civil War ended; the economy making an extremely tumultuous shift from agriculture to primary industry, new regions being populated, hundreds of new towns and cities being established. The education system had to attempt to deal with these changes while, at the same time, establishing an acceptable level of integrity.

The most important players in this effort were the teachers, the majority of whom had entered their profession fresh out of primary and secondary school owing to the lack of access to normal schools or to lack of the necessary prerequisites for entrance. Another major inhibitor was cost. Salaries for teachers, most of them women by this time, were the lowest in the professional ranks. Their situation obviously needed to be addressed in that education had traditionally been considered the foundation upon which the U.S. democracy rested.

8.2 The Problem of Measurement

A second major question that arose during this period was, "How can the individual student's level of ability actually be defined so that he or she can be provided with the most effective education?" While the question had been asked before, the approach now taken to answering it was made possible by advances in the scientific world.

The French government had been asking the same thing and had assigned a psychologist named Alfred Binet (1857–1911) to address the issue. Binet and his colleague, Theodore Simon, developed a set of questions to ask students that were not based on things learned at school but that focused on powers of observation, on memory powers, and on their problem-solving skills. From the answers received, Binet and Simon developed the concept of "mental age." They defined the subject's level of intellect by comparing his or her score to the average number of correct answers received from students at each age level.

In the United States, intelligence testing was introduced during World War I as a means of weeding out unfit recruits. The academic community adopted the new tool in 1917, owing to its effort to emulate industry and the accepted belief that measurement was the key to success. Originally, however, the tests devised were vague in their definition of "intelligence." They were also frequently biased, either intentionally or unintentionally, toward white Anglo-Saxon Protestants living in economically comfortable circumstances. In fact, their major purpose during the early days has been to provide a rationalization for racism and for social class differentiation. People from Black Africa, southern and eastern European nations didn't do as well on the test and, therefore, were deemed intellectually as well as socially inferior so that they were not pushed academically. Typically, they were place in the "general curriculum tract" and fed watered-down courses.

One of the leaders in the educational testing movement was the eventual developer of the Scholastic Aptitude Test (SAT), Carl Brigham, a Princeton professor who in 1923 published a study that ranked racial intelligence. At the top of the pile in this ranking dwelt northern Europeans. Below them came Eastern Europeans; then southern Europeans; and below them Black Africans. Brigham was against mixing these ethnic groups. He feared that such mixing would lower our population's overall level of intelligence. He proposed instituting stricter immigration laws to slow or stop the flow of those possessing what he defined as inferior intelligence into the country (Spring, pp. 267–269).

An argument was also made by supporters of ethnic profiling that intelligence is inherited and set. It could not be improved through education. They said that those with intelligence would learn what they needed to learn with minimum exposure. They said that trying to teach those who lacked adequate intelligence was a waste of time; that, in this latter case, emphasis should be on character building rather than on helping students grasp and remember subject matter they were incapable of grasping and remembering.

Though IQ became a topic of great interest, the ability to measure a student's intelligence did little to address the more comprehensive question of this period—how best to shape academic systems so that students could learn how to learn and could learn how to become productive contributors to the economy and to society—a question that had been central since the beginning of the Industrial Revolution.

Current academicians addressing this question once again divided into two camps with old agendas but new names. The "activity analysis camp" continued to espouse the mechanist philosophy. The most efficient ways to present material should be identified scientifically, then measured continuously for effectiveness so that on-going improvement was possible. For example, concerning spelling, researchers identified the 542 most commonly used words in the English language so that time would not be wasted learning words rarely spoken. Teachers should also be evaluated frequently in terms of their effectiveness and should receive periodic training. To support this training, a list of 83 major traits of good teachers was tabulated for them to study and attempt to emulate.

The "project relations camp" that opposed the activity analysis camp fed off the human relations school. It was represented by William Heard Kilpatrick (1871–1965), one of Dewey's students. Kilpatrick said, quite simply, that what a child learned was dependent on what that child found rewarding. This philosophy mirrored to a great extent the approach being introduced to the workplace by the previously mentioned social worker and management consultant, Mary Follett, that workers (students and teachers) had the same needs in the workplace (in the school) that they had at home; and by the previously mentioned researchers, Mayo and Roethlisberger, who showed through their work at Western Electric that employees (students) were more productive when directly involved in the decision-making (learning) process.

8.3 A Bump in the Road to Progress

The stock market crash of 1929 that precipitated the Great Depression changed how the United States as a nation

thought. It was caused mainly by greed and by too little regulation of banks and of brokerage firms. People started calling
for stronger financial controls and for a redistribution of the
nation's wealth through rewriting of the tax code. The education system suffered badly during the Depression; the amount
of funds flowing into it from tax monies decreased markedly.
Teachers were not paid; students went without food, sometimes without even water during their school day. Classes were
cancelled because schools had to lay off staff. The school year
was shortened.

Many of the leaders of the U.S. education movement like
Thomas Jefferson had visualized the sector as a shaper of
society. Teachers made an effort to play this role during the
Great Depression, to take the lead in shaping a new order.
They saw, better than most, the effect that the financial community's machinations with its laissez faire, "law of the jungle"
attitude had on the general public's welfare. The reaction from
the Robber Barons and their allies, however, was swift and
adamant. "Educators should do the job they were being paid
to do and stay out of politics. End of discussion." Most teachers faced with a choice between retaining their livelihood during such desperate times and leading a rebellion choose the
former. At the sametime they did what they could on a local
level to help relieve the suffering of their students—organizing
fund-raisers, donating part of their salaries, heading efforts to
bring food and clothing to the destitute.

During the first half of the 1900s, besides the Great
Depression, the United States went through World War I and
World War II, both of which also greatly affected the education system. For one thing, a shortage of teachers developed,
many choosing either to enlist in a branch of the military or
to take higher paying jobs in defense industries. At the same
time, science took on added importance. Government funds
began pouring into universities. Professors with training in
physics, chemistry, and other relevant fields began working on
defense contracts.

This swing toward the hard sciences was pronounced. In that the nation's survival was being threatened, the humanities were frequently treated as almost superfluous. Moreover, in order to survive, the nation's citizens had to pull together and put aside their differences, at least temporarily, teamwork becoming the rallying cry, and replacing the autocratic leadership style that had dominated the workplace for the past several decades. Input from all those involved was increasingly sought so that richer, more comprehensive solutions could be achieved.

This attitude spread to the education sector. The dominant voice of religion in policy and curriculum matters all but disappeared in the public system. It all but disappeared in a majority of colleges and universities as well. The business model for running school systems with a boss at the top of the hierarchy giving orders was replaced by a call for more input from teachers, parents, and, eventually, students.

The model for modern day colleges and universities was created during this period. So much new information and knowledge was being generated that academic studies had to be compartmentalized. Professors specialized in one area, continuing their education four additional years (the PhD) in order to become experts. Again following Germany's lead, research became increasingly important. But while in German universities "pure" research was encouraged—making advances that had no immediate practical value—in the United States the desire was to make discoveries that would be of immediate use, especially in the economic sector.

University graduate programs where students focused on one area of expertise, be it physics or economics or medicine or geography, became leaders in the new research-driven movement. As a result of this shift, professors took on a new role. Rather than just purveyors of existing knowledge, they now also became generators and explainers of new knowledge.

8.4 Teachers Unionize

Partially as a result of their new prestige and their elevated status during the late 1800s and early 1900s, professors began seeking more academic freedom, the right to present both sides of an argument along with their own opinions and the reasons supporting it. The industrial sector, however, from whence came most college and university trustees and a majority of the involved funding opposed this increased degree of empowerment. Industrial leaders wanted institutions of higher learning to focus, instead, on expanding research that served their purpose. They harkened back to the words of Charles Eliot, an earlier President of Harvard University, who in 1869 said that, "It is not the function of the teacher to settle philosophical and political controversies for the pupil, or even to recommend to him one set of opinions as better than any other. Exposition, not imposition of opinions is the professor's part" (Metzger, p. 126).

Those on the other side of the argument believed that the professor's main responsibility was to constantly seek and espouse the truth in social debates as well as in scientific matters regardless of the obstacles encountered. One incident that enflamed this controversy was the forced resignation of Professor Edward Ross from Stanford University due to his pro-labor rhetoric and activities. Partially as a result of this incident the American Association of University Professors (AAUP) was formed in 1915, its main charges being to fight for and protect academic freedom.

In the early 1900s, primary and secondary school teachers were also struggling to improve their situation, to increase their wage, to gain access to a retirement fund, and to gain job security in the form of seniority. As with labor unions, they had realized that the best way to make public school system administrators, along with the businessmen on school boards, along with politicians who sided with the businessmen, pay attention was to organize. For the most part, at least initially, they did not want to align themselves with traditional labor unions, reticent to give up control of their movement, wanting to keep the effort local and under their guidance. Those groups that did align, however, like the Chicago Federation of Teachers (CFT) which joined the Chicago Federation of Laborers (CFL), gained more political power and were able to address a broader range of issues so that eventually all teachers' unions followed suit.

The first issue addressed was pay, or the lack thereof. As a means of decreasing public expenditures during the scientific management era industrialists wanted to cut teacher wages. One of the mechanisms introduced to do so was the concept of "merit pay." Salary reductions would occur if teachers did not reach a level of performance set by bosses. This, of course, widened further the ideological divide between teachers and the administrators controlling their fate.

8.5 The National Education Association Becomes a Force

One of the responsibilities of the National Education Association (NEA) formed, as has been said, in 1857, was to represent and defend the interests of primary and secondary school teachers. By 1870, the organization included four policy-making divisions that dealt with normal schools, higher education, superintendency, and elementary education. Originally, the NEA was run by an "old boy" clique. Although the majority of primary and secondary school teachers by this time were females none were elected or appointed to leadership positions. In 1917, the organization moved to Washington and began strengthening its relationship with government agencies. One of the eventual outcomes of this effort was the idea of providing federal aid for public education. Another was the beginning of efforts to create a separate Federal Department of Education.

In the early days of the NEA's existence, regional and national meetings were organized in major cities. Each attendant to such meetings received one vote on policy decisions. The problem with this arrangement, however, was one of location. The city sponsoring the meeting could more easily pack it and sway the vote. The alternative decided upon was for each state to elect and send delegates to regional and national meetings. At first these delegates were voted for, but in 1920, the vote was eliminated and delegates were appointed by district administrators (males), the majority of them, not surprisingly, being male district administrators. Teachers as representatives, for the most part, were excluded. Once again, the situation in the education sector mirrored that found in the industrial sector where all-male boards of directors formulated policy with no input from the workers. Once again it was an "old-boy" network.

This situation prevailed until the 1950s when the NEA was blamed for the decline of the public education system, for the system falling behind those of countries we were competing with economically. On the basis of these charges, the federal government became increasingly involved in formulating policy through the Department of Education.

8.6 A Battle for Survival

During the Great Depression, besides trying to cut teacher salaries, an ongoing effort in the business community, spearheaded by the Chamber of Commerce, was made to cut back on other portions of school funding. In order to do this, the Chamber recommended, among other things, the elimination of clubs, sports (at least some), kindergarten, and night classes. It recommended cutting the number of classes offered, cutting the length of the school day, and adding more students to classes. Eventually turning the tables, protectors of the system began blaming the business community, particularly banks and brokerage firms, for creating the problem in the first place, suggesting that they had failed in their responsibility to shape a healthy economy, suggesting that the education sector should, at this point, take the lead in instituting the changes necessary to economic revival.

An educational philosophy named "social reconstruction" that encouraged this approach was introduced by a teacher named George Counts in a 1932 speech entitled, "Dare Schools Build a New Social Order?" He said that schools should lead the effort, that school boards should focus on the needs of children and the community rather than on the desires of industry. The NEA supported Counts' proposal, though the organization took no steps to implement his ideas. Eventually, an academic journal called *Social Frontier* was published focusing on three major themes. First, that capitalism had failed to fully use science and technology for the benefit of humanity. Second, that the capitalistic system with its profit motive had a negative effect on individual morality. Third, that the current economic order in the United States created economic insecurity for large groups of people (Bowers, p. 24).

The response of the Chamber of Commerce and the business community was predictable. Cries of "Communism!" and "Socialism!" rang out, these being the concepts that the U.S. public had, by this time, been programmed to fear. So, while very little changed during all this economic tumult, though the public school system failed to mobilize and lead the desired movement toward social and economic reconstruction, the period and movement helped cement the image of educators as being liberal, as being in favor of generating social progress along with economic progress.

8.7 A Slow Recovery

Eventually, the depression subsided. World War II helped revitalize the economy. The education community received a large boost when *The GI Bill of Rights* (1944) was passed by Congress paying for veterans to attend college. Whereas middle managers had previously learned most of what they needed to know on-the-job, new students now graduated with most of the required skills already in their repertoire, saving companies time and money.

But while colleges and universities were doing well following World War II, the lower levels of the education hierarchy continued to struggle. The shortage of teachers at primary and secondary schools remained serious, owing largely to the relatively low amount of pay offered. Veterans, after going back to college, opted for higher paying jobs in the rapidly growing industrial sector that also provided greater opportunity for advancement.

Most primary and secondary school teachers were still being trained in two-year normal schools at this point. In the mid-1900s, however, a solution was found that enhanced the training provided. Normal schools were converted to four-year teacher's colleges funded by state government. Tuition was relatively cheap at state teachers colleges, but in return students had to sign a contract promising to teach for at least two year upon graduation. The major problem faced during this transition was that those hired initially by the state system as instructors in state teachers colleges lacked the necessary theoretical background and were forced to depend mainly on their experience when shaping curriculum. The situation, of course, improved as increasing amounts of research were conducted and as an increasing number of graduates returned to teach. Also, training for future college-level professors, based on the Columbia University model, was now being offered by a growing number of private institutions around the country, the University of Chicago and Stanford University developing outstanding reputations, especially in terms of research.

Curriculum at the primary and secondary levels continued to be based largely on the recommendations made by The Committee of Ten in the early 1890s. In 1918, the Commission on the Reorganization of Secondary Education added "The Seven Cardinal Principles." The assignment given by this Commission was to update the education philosophy and objectives for secondary education. Swinging back toward the human relations approach, the Commission urged that a new emphasis be adopted, one that would take into account individual differences, goals, attitudes, and abilities.

The Seven Cardinal Principles of Secondary Education according to the Commission included the following:

- Health—Students should be encouraged to practice good health habits. Teachers should provide good role models. Schools should be equipped with the space and equipment necessary for health-improving activities.
- Command of Fundamental Processes—Student should be well grounded in the fundamentals—writing, reading, oral and written expression, and mathematics. New textbooks and approaches to teaching these subjects needed to be developed.
- Worthy Home Membership—Education should shape students to be "worthy" members of a family and society. The subjects contributing to this effort should include literature, music, social studies, and art. Males and females who attend the same school should attempt to get along.
- Vocational Training—Students should work on understanding themselves and what they are interested in doing with their lives. They should be exposed to a variety of career possibilities so that they choose wisely when the time comes. They should understand the role various occupations play in the community, the contribution each makes.
- Civic Education—Students should develop an awareness of and a concern for their community. They should belong to organizations that serve the community, working with others, functioning effectively as members of a group or groups.

- Worthwhile Use of Leisure Time—Students should use their leisure time to further enrich their body, their mind, their spirit, and their personality. Schools should provide activities that encourage them to do so such as sports, drama clubs, and choral groups.
- Ethical Character—Teachers should instill in students an understanding of personal responsibility and initiative. (Raubinger, Rowe, Piper, West. *The Development of Secondary Education*).

The Commission emphasized that these principles did not stand alone, but were interdependent. Obviously, however, while they were useful in largely the same way that the Ten Commandments are useful, while they set the tone, The Seven Cardinal Principles contributed little by way of improving the education model or by way of up-dating curriculum, so that by the end of World War II, in light of the societal changes that had occurred, the need for another reevaluation of the education system was apparent.

8.8 Again, How to Deal with the Poor

An issue that reasserted itself during this period, the one that had existed since the beginning of the U.S.'s education efforts, that had been especially important during periods of mass immigration, was how to deal with the poor. The prevailing logic during the 1960s was that, owing to the environment, poor people were born into, grew up in, and usually remained trapped in for the rest of their lives, any contribution they might originally have been able to make never materialized. In turn, their children were trapped in the same lifestyle, thus perpetuating the cycle of poverty. Also, with advances in technology, with increasingly sophisticated machinery and systems being incorporated into the workplace, the level of education required to be productive was rising, leaving the poor even further behind.

In 1964, President Johnson, following the lead of President Kennedy who started the war on poverty, signed the *Economic Opportunity Act* creating, among other things, Head Start, a program that worked with pre-kindergarteners from impoverished families on the fundamentals of education in an effort to provide them with an equal opportunity to succeed once they entered the public school system. Other programs funded by the Act included the Job Corps, created to give teenagers the skills necessary to hold a job; Community Development programs; funding for school libraries; funding for text books and instructional materials; funding for research focused on meeting the educational needs of the poor; funding to strengthen state departments of education so they might play a major role in the effort. Education, in the minds of those driving the effort, was the key to breaking the cycle of poverty. It could play a major role in shaping or reshaping the mindset of the poor beginning at a young age so that rather than being a drain on the economy, they might eventually contribute to it.

Chapter 9

Segregation, Deculturalization, Assimilation: A Sad Chapter in the History of U.S. Public Education

9.1 The Lingering Legacy of Slavery in the United States

The concept of "segregation," which involved an effort to exclude the members of different races that had immigrated to or had been brought to the United States against their will, helped shape the nation's approach to education during the 1800s and early 1900s. The founding fathers clearly stated their belief that the U.S. population should be predominantly White and Protestant, and that the education system should support supremacy of this group. However, almost from the beginning, there was the problem of Black slaves, especially in the South, and what to do with them in terms of schooling.

Before the Civil War, most White children from southern families who attended school were enrolled in private academies. The children of Afro-Americans who were either slaves or tenant farmers received no formal education. Attempts by slaves to teach themselves informally were, in most cases, strongly discouraged, with the penalties for trying to learn to read including whippings and, in some instances, death.

Owners did not want their slaves to gain education for three reasons. First, slaves were critical to the agricultural economy. They worked in the fields cultivating and harvesting the cotton, the tobacco, and the vegetables grown, providing a majority of the physical labor required. Gaining education might encourage them to want to improve their economic situation, to seek other work, and to demand payment for their labor. Second, African-Americans eventually outnumbered Whites in many southern states. One of the greatest fears of the White community was an organized uprising, several of which did occur. If kept ignorant, slaves would be easier to control. It would be more difficult for them to organize. Third, slave owners usually belonged to extremely religious communities. Obviously, the concept of slavery went against foundational teachings of Christianity. This problem was dealt with by relegating slaves to the status of less-than-human, their role being the same as that of other lower level animals—to serve their masters. If slaves showed they could be educated in a human fashion, and that they could learn as easily as Whites, the rationalization would no longer hold and slave owners, as true Christians, would be forced to deal with the resultant guilt.

Following the Civil War, Afro-Americans, with the assistance from northern educators, worked to establish a public school system. This system initially took in more Black students than White students. Whites who dominated the state political systems, however, began passing discriminatory laws barring Blacks from taking part in classes. Their reasoning was that the economy remained predominantly agricultural and the ex-slaves were needed in the fields.

As the situation continued to deteriorate, some Black leaders accepted this second-class status for their people as a
compromise that both Whites and Black could live with. It was
eventually agreed that Black students would receive education in the basics, in things useful to the menial types of work
they would end up doing, but nothing more. Under this new
arrangement, because what they needed in terms of education
was obviously different from what White students needed, it
was decided that Afro-Americans should be enrolled in different schools with a less-demanding curriculum. Thus, the segregated White–Black public school system was born. While in
1875, shortly after the war, the per-capita government expendi-
ture per Black student was higher than that for White student,
by 1900, it was four to five times higher for Whites. Moreover,
by 1875, owing to the efforts by powerful Southern planters,
government funding for the expansion of the Black public
school system stopped while the population of Black children
continued to grow (Spring, p. 185).

In the early 1900s, the system of Black public schools again
began expanding in the South, with most of the funds for this
expansion came from the Black community and from private
philanthropic foundations such as the Anna T. Jeanes Fund
and the Julius Rosenwald Fund. Blacks were forced to continue paying taxes that were fed mainly into the White public
education sector while, at the same time, donating their own
monies to build schools and pay teachers in the Black sector.

9.2 Deculturalization and Assimilation as Alternatives

Diametrically opposed to the tactic of segregation, "deculturalization" and "assimilation" tactics also helped shape U.S.
education during the 1800s and early 1900s. Another sad note
in the annals of U.S. history is the attempt by the Federal
Government during that period to deculturalize and assimilate

Native Americans. Tribes that had been forced out of the east and across mid-America's plains by settlers were running out of places to retreat to. The concept of "manifest destiny" made clear the intention of the steady stream of immigrants who were arriving, mainly from Europe, to fill the country coast to coast. This left only two alternatives for the Native American population—to be wiped out or to be assimilated.

After a major portion of the Native American population had, indeed, been wiped out by war with better-armed U.S. soldiers but more so by diseases introduced by the settlers, government emphasis switched to assimilation. Schools were used to eradicate the tribal traditions that students had grown up with and to reprogram the students to be good Christians and good Americans. One of the techniques used was to remove children entirely from their families and tribes at a young age and to ship them to boarding schools in other parts of the country where they were not allowed to speak their native language, where they raised the U.S. flag every morning and recited the pledge of allegiance, where they studied for half the day, then labored during the other half on the school farm as a means of acquiring a useful trade, and as a way to learn the value of hard work. Only in 1928 was the practice of deculturalization stopped, following the publication of the *Meriam Report* on *The Problems of Indian Administration.* As a result of report findings, efforts begun to return students to their reservations and to allow them to receive their education in a reservation school.

Concerning Mexican-Americans, after the U.S. military under President Polk invaded Texas in 1846 and then occupied areas to the west, including New Mexico and California, the Mexicans who had not been driven out were treated largely with disdain. They were used as poorly paid farm laborers. As railroads linked this region more closely with the rest of the nation during the late 1800s, agriculture grew increasingly important. Cheap Mexican labor gained the same economic value that slave labor had held in the Deep South. Again, segregated public schools were put into place for Mexican-Americans using second-hand books passed down from the White schools. The main responsibility of these schools was to "Americanize" their students. English was the required language of instruction. The only schools where students were allowed to speak Spanish were those controlled by the Catholic Church. Although national laws had been passed by this time regarding attendance, the Mexican children were not required to show up, and often did not show up, preferring instead to work in the fields as a means of earning money for their families.

When Chinese immigrants began arriving during the 1850s gold rush in California, they also had to deal with segregation. The children of those who stayed to work as laborers in farm fields or to help build the transcontinental railroad were not allowed to attend California public schools. Eventually, this law was contested. As a result, the state opened separate, segregated schools for Chinese students, as had been done previously with the Afro-American population. The same thing happened to Japanese immigrants who began arriving during the early 1900s. Unrestricted access to the public schools system for Chinese, Japanese, and Koreans was not legislated until after World War II.

9.3 The Battle to Eliminate Segregation

Previous legal support for segregationist attitudes can be traced to a Supreme Court ruling in the 1895 case of a Louisiana man one-eighth Black who was arrested for riding in a White train compartment and refusing to move to the Black compartment. The Court in that situation ruled that if the facilities for both races were equal, the man, Homer Plessy, had no legal grounds for his complaint. Thus, the doctrine of "separate but equal" was born, supporting the argument of the segregationists and becoming their rallying cry.

But while the Black and White education systems were kept separate, they were not, in most cases, anywhere close to being equal. This was because the monies raised for education through taxes were distributed by local governments and school boards. Blacks rarely, if ever, were elected to positions as officials in small southern towns and large northern cities. The economy of the South was still suffering from the Civil War while northern cities were being overrun by immigrants. There was not enough money to meet all the educational needs. Thus, Black schools frequently lacked the funds to purchase adequate furnishings (desks, tables, etc.), equipment, and books.

But in 1954, with the *Brown versus Board of Education of Topeka* ruling by the U.S. Supreme Court, the concept of separate but equal was overthrown. This was a case in which the Afro-American plaintiff was seeking permission to attend an all-White public school close to her home instead of traveling to a distant Black school. The court ruled that her rights as a citizen were being infringed upon by the segregationist attitude of the community. The ruling was based on the court's interpretation of the Fourteenth Amendment of the Constitution which says that "No State shall make or enforce any law which shall abridge the privileges or immunities of citizens...nor...deprive any person of life, liberty, or property, without due process of law; nor deny to any person within its jurisdiction the equal protections of the law."

With this ruling, Afro-American children gained access to any school they wished to attend. The problem was now one of law implementation. No way existed, at least initially, to enforce this freedom of choice. Black schools were located in Black neighborhoods. White schools were located in White neighborhoods. Very few parents or children were willing to journey through hostile territory in order to reach a destination where it had been made clear that they were not welcome.

It took the Civil Rights Movement during the 1950s and 1960s led by the NAACP with Dr. Martin Luther King as chief spokesperson to get things headed in the right direction. Nonviolent protests spread through the country, such protests turning violent only when racists attacked with fists, clubs, dogs, and fire hoses. It took national coverage by the media, films of those marches and assaults being broadcast across the country using recently developed communications technology, to educate the public as to what was going on, to allow citizens to view it almost immediately on their televisions, to goad the government to action in terms of enforcing school integration.

In 1964, Congress passed the Civil Rights Act. The most important part of this act involved the distribution of government funds throughout the public education sector. In order to receive these funds, or to continue receiving these funds, schools had to discontinue their discriminatory practices. The Federal Government also funded and implemented a busing system to carry Black students to what had previously been all-White schools and White students to what had previously been all-Black schools. Again, there were problems. White students and their parents complained that the new Black students were behind academically, that they had too much catching up to do, and that the White students were not progressing as rapidly as they could, or should. Black students complained that the White teachers ignored them.

In the Deep South, many Whites considered the Civil Rights Act and its consequences unacceptable. Their solution was to open private schools, most of them church related. Not being part of the public school system and not receiving government funding, these schools could shape their student population and curriculum any way they wanted to. Thus, the public school system in the South became largely Black.

Owing to the expense incurred by the White private schools and those attending, supporters began lobbying for access to a portion of the tax monies they had paid to support the public system. Partially as a result of this lobbying, the idea for what would eventually be called the "voucher system" emerged. Initially, the plan called for underprivileged students to be given a monetary voucher to pay for their education. They could cash this voucher in at any school they chose, thus making them more attractive as students. The system could also improve the quality of education provided, because schools would compete for the vouchers. The proposal was then advanced that the entire population of students—Black, White, Hispanic, Asian—should receive vouchers to pay for their education, individuals being allowed to cash them at any public or private school they wished.

Another concept that emerged during this period in an effort to encourage peaceful desegregation was the concept of "magnet schools." These were created at the secondary level and could be attended in place of traditional public high schools. Students had to apply, be interviewed, and to be accepted. Each magnet school focused on one area of learning such as the arts (theater, dance, and music), or the sciences (physics, chemistry, and biology), or engineering. With this approach, the schools hoped to break down traditional racial barriers by attracting more serious students with similar interests who were dedicated to making progress in their desired field, who desired to interact with like-minded students regardless of race.

The magnet school approach, however, though successful in attracting students, though successful in desegregation efforts, went against the philosophy that had dominated academic thinking in the United States for more than 200 years—that the key to economic and societal success was to offer students at primary and secondary school levels a well-balanced curriculum, including all subjects considered important. The question that needed to be asked, therefore, was which approach—magnet school or traditional—produced the best long-term results? Or, perhaps more importantly, could the strengths of the two approaches somehow be combined?

9.4 Following the Lead of the Black Community

Encouraged by the refusal of Blacks to back down in their quest for equality, other minorities began campaigning to improve their situation as well. Native Americans rebelled against continuing efforts, despite the Meriam Report's findings, to deculturize them, to absorb them into the Anglo-Protestant culture. "Termination policies" enacted during the late 1940s and early 1950s dissolved tribes, shut down reservations, and relocated Native Americans into cities. Following the example of the Afro-Americans, leaders of the Native American tribes came together in 1961 at the American Indian Chicago Conference and spoke out against the termination policies.

After being elected to the U.S. Presidency in 1960, John F. Kennedy sided with these leaders. A Task Force on Indian Affairs was formed under the Department of the Interior. The purpose was to give Native Americans a stronger voice in decisions affecting them. One such decision concerned control over the education of their children, the ability to include lessons pertaining to the preservation of their culture in the school curriculum. *The Indian Self-Determination and Education Assistance Act* of 1975 gave tribes this control, gave them the legal right to design, and run their own education programs.

The main rationalization offered at this point for segregating Mexican-Americans, for putting them in their own schools, was that they had special education needs; that they needed to learn English before they could progress on to other subjects. In 1946, a U.S. District Court judge in California ruled that segregation was illegal in that it impeded Mexican-American students in their efforts to learn English. When similar rulings were made in other states, those against integrating the classroom fought back by redrawing the school districting boundaries along cultural lines and distributing tax funds unequally. Such battles have continued into modern times, as have the battles to allow equal access to the education system for the handicapped.

As the various minority groups garnered increasing support in their quest for equal educational opportunity, another related issue began to gain momentum. This was the call for bilingual schooling. Mexican-Americans argued that courses should be offered in Spanish as well as English; that Spanish food should be served in cafeterias; that more Spanish-speaking teachers should be hired by public schools. Native Americans joined the movement calling for courses teaching their language. Emphasis was on developing a stronger sense of identity, a stronger sense of cultural pride in minority students. Emphasis was on having all students recognize that the minority cultures represented in the academic community were just as important as the dominant Anglo-Protestant one.

Eventually, it was proposed that a system of alternative, ethnocentric schools should be opened, each one focusing on an individual culture, teaching from that culture's perspective. The opponents of such bilingual and multi-cultural education, however, argued that if you did this for one minority group others would have the legal right to demand the same special treatment and that the United States would end up with an aggregate of education approaches rather than one comprehensive system that gave students the skills required to contribute to society as a whole. They also argued that the nation needed one culture by which to define itself, that other cultures were welcome, should be allowed to coexist if they didn't try to take over, that parts of other cultures could be absorbed into the mother culture, but that the major emphasis should remain on ensuring that all citizens, no matter what their background, gained the universal underpinnings necessary to function effectively.

Arthur Schlesinger Jr, a well-known historian who was writing at the time, shared his belief that the nation's core values had been generated by its White, Anglo-Protestant traditions, and that these core values should be the foundation upon which all school curriculum was built. English had been the language through which these values were given voice. Therefore, every student in the public school system should be required to learn English as the appropriate language for understanding the democratic principles upon which the nation's culture rested. As a result of these sentiments, several states proceeded to make English their official language, thus requiring that all schools in the system used it when teaching (Spring, pp. 380–381).

Chapter 10

The New Kid on the Block

10.1 From Humble Beginnings

Beginning in 1877 with the invention of the phonograph as a means of recording and repeating sound, technology assumed a role in the evolution of education theory that would eventually revolutionize it. Soon after the invention of the phonograph, the contributions of a number of scientists from different countries led to the development of the motion picture camera, motion picture film, and the projection system. While the phonograph did not create much of a stir in the education community, the advent of motion pictures triggered a highly emotional debate concerning what their content should be and who should make the involved decisions.

Four different factions were involved in this debate. First, private sector investors and entrepreneurs argued against the imposition of constraints saying that regulation of the new industry would go against the First Amendment of the United States Constitution; that it would infringe upon freedom of speech as well as freedom of the press. They said that regulation would also contradict the concept of free enterprise, the driving force behind economic development during that period.

The second faction was the religious establishment led by the Catholic Church that feared movies would have too strong influence on the minds and morals of parishioners, especially the young, and that movies would lead parishioners astray, diverting their attention from the important things in life.

The third faction, the education community, feared that movies would fill the minds of students with misinformation, would take time away from their studies, drawing attention away from important subject matter and focusing it on trivia. Some educators, however, also realized the potential value of films as a teaching vehicle. Comparative studies conducted in the early 1900s indicated that films were far more effective than books or lectures in teaching factual information and that the information learned in this manner was retained longer (Noble, p. 420).

The fourth faction was the government, which would be responsible for imposing restrictions on the new industry, if required. Other studies were conducted. These studies supported the formulation of such restrictions by showing that movies were disrupters of sleep patterns in children; that movies affected attitude, grades, and the ability to pay attention in class due to daydreaming; that movies encouraged the development of precocious sexual behavior.

To counter this negative publicity, a recommendation was made by the film industry that movie appreciation courses be offered in public schools; these courses eventually including the use of industry-provided study guides for the films being watched. A committee of educators and religious leaders was formed to rate movies and eliminate those that might be considered unacceptable. One reported result of this approach was that students who took the course began reading more and were interested in the books from which screenplays were adapted. Teachers, pleased by this phenomenon, began encouraging students to attend more movies.

As the movie industry continued to grow and attract greater numbers of customers, its leaders acknowledged publicly their power to spread ideas throughout society and the ethical responsibility such power carried. They also realized that if they did not take the involved obligation seriously, leaders from the religious and education communities would force government to step in. So the movie industry decided to self-regulate, putting into place a production code that required movies to teach audiences "moral, political, and social lessons." A list of *Don'ts and Be Carefuls* was distributed throughout the industry. Then, in 1930, a *Code to Govern the Making of Talking, Synchronized and Silent Pictures* was adopted.

Religious factions played a large role in the writing of this code. One of the major concerns for those involved was the difficulty in limiting who would be allowed to watch a movie. This, of course, was not a problem in the classroom where the teacher could select and preview films, where audience members were all of the same age. The remaining problem in the classroom was of cost. When no funds were available, teachers would encourage students to read the study guide in class, then to view the film at the local cinema.

The code was taken very seriously. Movies should teach the right values, the right behaviors. They should in no way aggrandize evil, wrongdoing, or unethical behavior. The good guys always had to win; the bad guys always had to end up being punished. Despite the tribulations endured by characters as the plot progressed, endings were always positive. Societal problems were either not presented or were "spun" to give them a positive, uplifting connotation. In 1946, Walt Disney Productions released *Song of the South*, an extremely popular musical featuring an old, Black slave, Uncle Remus, who told tales about how Br'er Rabbit, a sassy fellow, continually outwitted Br'er Fox and Br'er Bear to the young son of the plantation owner. Everybody happy, everybody smiling, and Uncle Remus, in the movie, seemed quite content in his role as a slave, instructing the young master as to how good always triumphs over evil.

10.2 The Radio Takes Center Stage

The next shock in terms of the impact of technology on education came with the advent of the radio in the early 1900s. Now students didn't have to travel to the movie house and pay money to be distracted from their studies; they could be distracted right in their own homes by just flicking the "on" switch and turning the tuning dial. Again controversy raged. Should the radio remain a private-sector phenomenon supported by advertising, or should the government control and support it with tax revenues as in Great Britain? If it remained in the private sector, would the U.S. culture be reshaped in a negative manner by the advertising that supported it?

The industry argued that their educational effort reached thousands of listeners of all ages and that, instead of "experts" dictating what the public listened to on the radio, people should be able to make their own choices from a variety of alternatives; this was the democratic approach. The Federal Communications Commission (FCC) was formed in 1934 in part to deal with this controversy. It then created a Federal Radio Education Committee to provide expertise on educational programming and to conduct research on listener tastes. But until the government decided to provide funding, radio had to continue supporting itself and, like any other free-market business, was dependent on sales to do so (in this case advertising). It had to "follow the dollar."

This necessity led radio stations to shape some programming in ways that segments of the population found unacceptable, the major culprit being violence on shows children had access to—actors getting shot, beaten up, murdered. Parent groups, religious groups, school groups, politicians began protesting, so that the FCC was forced to step in and warn that if stations didn't cut down on that sort of programming, the FCC would find ways to punish them, going even so far as to revoke their broadcasting license.

Eventually, the radio industry followed the example of the movie industry and instituted self-censorship codes that address two priorities—programming for children and the types of advertising accepted. In terms of programming for children, emphasis was on creating heroes to be worshiped, heroes who would encourage good values, colorful heroes who were incorruptible and who always won.

10.3 And, Then, Television Hits the Scene

The next technology to impact the education sector was television. First demonstrated at Philadelphia's Franklin Institute in 1934, televisions began appearing in homes across the nation during the 1940s. This new communications technology combined the benefits of movies and radio. It was a visual experience like movies but, at the same time, it offered sound, came directly into the home, and was relatively inexpensive after the necessary equipment had been purchased. Once again, the private sector versus government control argument erupted, those against allowing stations to provide whatever kind of programming sold best saying that a "vast wasteland" devoid of meaningful, instructive, or useful content had been created, that a majority of what was offered contributed little to the betterment of individuals and society.

Once again, in 1967, a commission was formed at the national level to study the issue. It was called The Carnegie Commission on Educational Television. One of its successes, from the education point of view, was the eventual creation of the Corporation for Public Broadcasting. The Carnegie Commission emphasized the use of television for informal education reaching audiences of all ages. It also took up the challenge of educating preschoolers and the under-privileged.

Out of this effort came *The Children's Television Workshop* (1968), a publicly funded project, and *Sesame Street*, The Workshop's first and most successful program. The Workshop's creators decided to present in an amusing manner a vision of the world as it ought to be, trying to encourage a positive approach to life using a wide range of child-friendly hand puppets to do so.

Thus, the ongoing argument between those against public funding for our education system and those who saw such an investment as valuable to the nation's future, an investment that pays back big time, an investment that is critical to our economic success, shifted once again to favor the pro-investment camp. Gerald Lesser, a professor of education and developmental psychology at Harvard who became involved in The Children's Television Workshop, stated his belief that education through television could be superior to that delivered by a teacher in the classroom because it was entertaining, because children did not have to deal with the threat of failure and humiliation, because children could control the learning process by simply flicking the on–off switch or changing channels (Lesser, pp. 88–89).

10.4 The Computer Makes a New Education Paradigm Possible

The next and most important advance in technology in terms of reshaping education, the potential of which this book explores, was the computer, developed during the early 1940s. In a way, the computer completed the progression. With movies, students could see the things that words in books portrayed—what the streets of Paris looked like during the French Revolution; a ship full of immigrants on their way to the United States; a pyramid in ancient Egypt; a woodland-bounded colonial homestead in the 1600s, and so on. Then the radio arrived to give access to great amounts of verbal information, different stations offering different programs to the listener. Next, television combined the visual and verbal, again offering a variety of programs the viewer could choose from, television becoming, as many said, society's third educational force after the family and the school.

But the computer differed from its predecessors in several important ways. First, it allowed users to learn what they wanted to learn, choosing from an almost endless range of subjects. As part of this, the computer gave users access to just about any data or information available in a specific subject area. Computers allowed users to manipulate the information being accessed. Computers allowed them to shape the delivery of their lesson—written, verbal, visual—then to modify and combine these modes. In essence the computer gave learners almost total control of a vastly accelerated, nonthreatening (computers didn't laugh at your mistakes or punish you with poor grades) learning process. At the same time, computers allowed people to create new knowledge by manipulating the information they were given access to.

People could educate themselves by watching movies or by listening to radio programs or tapes of radio programs or by watching television. But, in these instances, their control of the process was limited. To become well versed in any subject took a much longer time. Also, the lesson received through these media was fixed. Also, in terms of testing how much had been learned, radio and television could ask questions about the lesson, but could not grade answers, could not provide feedback, and could not give the test over.

The computer could do all of these things.

Historically, the philosophy of education has centered around two major questions. The first is "What should be taught?" The second is "How should the lesson best be delivered?" In terms of what should be taught, over time a list of subjects evolved in academic circles with no real concern for what the students might want to focus on, at least during their primary and secondary years of education. This list eventually included mathematics, English, history, foreign language, science, and geography. The range of materials developed by publishers and used by teachers for these lessons has varied greatly according to their biases. For example, should history tell what really happened, or focus on instilling a sense of national pride? Should teachers portray the War with Mexico as a land grab by the U.S. government, or focus on the bravery of the men defending the Alamo? More recently, should the Vietnamese War be portrayed as a brave attempt to stop the spread of communism in Southeast Asia? Or should it be portrayed as a war the United States lost, and questions asked as to why it was fought and lost? In terms of English, what novels should be used to represent a certain period of literature? Concerning healthcare, should methods of birth control be discussed or not?

While, through these years, emphasis has been on standardization of curriculum, on getting teachers to shape their lessons in the same manner in order to "level the playing field," the effort can go only so far. In some ways this limitation is a good thing. Education is a product of culture and culture cannot, probably should not, be totally standardized. Education prepares students to live in a specific culture; it helps students understand what is required and what is possible in that culture. But what is required and what is possible might vary from region to region, from school to school. Alternatives should also be explored.

In terms of the method of delivery, instruction, up to this point, has been presented verbally by the teacher with the assistance of hornbooks, textbooks, workbooks, blackboards, auditory tapes, films, televisions, and CDs. The teacher has decided which vehicle or vehicles to use. With the advent of computers, however, all this, as has been said, is about to change. The student will be able to control both the "What should be taught?" question and the "How should the lesson best be delivered?" question to a much greater extent.

Chapter 11

Education in the United States during the Mid- to Late 1900s

11.1 Still Trying to Figure Out the Best Approach

During the 1950s and 1960s not much changed in the design of the U.S. public education system. *The Elementary and Secondary Education Act* was passed in 1965 during the Lyndon B. Johnson presidency (1963–1969) as part of the poverty program. It served mainly as a funding initiative to improve the caliber of education at these levels and to ensure equal access to education opportunity. The teaching process at that time was fairly automatic with little room for innovation by instructors and especially by students.

Eventually, sociologists and psychologists began attacking the system, saying that it failed to cover much of the spectrum of students' needs; that individuality was lost, but equally important, that the system had created its own reality, one which isolated students from the reality it was supposed to be preparing them for. While during the early 1900s schools had been seen as a haven for the young rescued from the drudgery and danger of factory work, they were now seen as too protective, as failing to prepare students for their life afterward.

The Panel on Youth, part of President Nixon's Science Advisory Committee addressed this situation in 1973. Its report, *Youth: Transition to Adulthood,* mirrored the above complaints, listing what it considered to be areas in the current system that needed improvement, sometimes also suggesting remedies. The report reiterated the belief that the system isolated students from adults and the adult world. No direct remedy, however, was suggested for this perceived shortcoming.

The panel was also against age segregation, against defining grade levels by age, saying that students lost out by not interacting with students of different ages, especially with older ones. Another weakness of the system, according to the report, was that education and work were not integrated. First, students gained their education; then, after their education was completed, students found jobs. The panel suggested a work–study approach that allowed students to hold part-time jobs while receiving their formal education. The minimum wage should be lowered so that employers would be encouraged to hire young people. At the same time, in support of this idea, the panel questioned both the concept of compulsory school attendance and child labor laws, saying the involved laws restrained young people from choosing activities they might be better suited for. The panel also recommended that continual education be made available even after people entered the workforce.

When one listens to the criticisms and recommendations coming from the Panel on Youth, it sounds as though members were trying to revert to the Industrial Revolution mentality concerning education. Their mind-set seemed to support "human-capital theory," that the value of education should be measured primarily in terms of its economic return. One reason for this attitude was that most of the U.S. Presidents during those years were Republicans—Richard Nixon, Gerald Ford, Ronald Reagan, George H. W. Bush—and the Republican Party was still clinging tenaciously to the laissez faire economics approach, measuring just about everything in terms of economic return.

The part of the report about the lack of connect between students and the real world did have some credence in the public education system. However, though I doubt that the panel had this in mind, its major impact, as we have seen from modern history, was to bring to light a serious and eventually dangerous flaw in the thriving private school system, a flaw that has played a major role in this country's social upheaval.

11.2 The Problem with Private Schools: The Bubble World

Private school students were usually relatively wealthy. They were educated and reached maturity in a comfortable bubble where their socialization and the quality of education received gave them a feeling of superiority. From there these students progress onto another bubble world, frequently an Ivy League school, with its class debates and guest lecturers and heavy workload, where again they were sheltered from the real world, developing their own culture, their own network, their own code of behavior. Private school students read about the real world, studied it theoretically, decided how it should be shaped, but never really got slapped around by it.

Quite possibly, this is what the panel was talking about, or should have been talking about, such sentiments being far better suited to the private school system than the public. Many students in the public high school system held part-time jobs to help support their families; and a majority of students in the state college system did so in order to help pay tuition. Students in the private school system, on the other hand, rarely held jobs, or rarely left the bubble. Rather, these students spent their time studying and socializing; they spent their time developing the belief that they understood more than the average Joe, and that because of their superior education they should be the leaders, the ones making the decisions.

And so, following graduations, these students moved into jobs, frequently in government, where they gain the authority to make decisions with major implications from the real world. Unfortunately, too many of them carried their bubble world along, gathering bubble world buddies around them for reinforcement.

In 1947, the CIA was formed to combat the spread of Russia's influence in Europe following World War II. Many idealistic Ivy Leaguers rushed to join its ranks. The agency's most noted director was Allen Dulles, a Princeton graduate, who created a reality for the agency that differed greatly from that of the U.S. government to which he supposedly reported. According to the book *Legacy of Ashes: A History of the CIA* by Tim Weiner, Dulles distorted facts, lied to Congress and to the president, supported covert operations he was told not to support, spent funds he was told not to spend and, in the process, got thousands of people killed, owing largely to his miscalculations and his bubble-bred arrogance.

Eventually, the United States became involved in the Vietnamese War, labeled by many the Harvard War. The bubble team that began and ran that war included Harvard graduates and teachers, including President John F. Kennedy, Secretary of Defense Robert McNamara, National Security Advisor Henry Kissinger, and National Security Advisor McGeorge Bundy. The major reason given for going to war was the *domino effect*, that if South Vietnam fell to communism, the movement would sweep from there westward across Cambodia, Thailand, and Burma to India.

Following the death of over 10,000 U.S. soldiers and hundreds of thousands of civilians, South Vietnam did fall to the Vietcong. But instead of marching onward, the victors spent their time consolidating the nation and turning it into one of the world's fastest growing economies. Why did the involved U.S. leaders feel the need to go to war? Why didn't they listen to people with real experience in that part of the world? Did their bubble world education have anything to do with their obvious lack of insight? One might suspect so.

More recently, we have the Iraq and Afghanistan Wars, this time labeled the Yale Wars. Graduates and Yale faculty members inside the bubble who ran and supported this war include President George W. Bush; Vice President Richard Cheney, who, though he flunked out, maintained his contacts; Deputy Secretary of Defense Paul Wolfowitz; and Paul Bremmer, U.S. Administrator to Iraq. Once again the reason given for attacking these two countries turned out to be false; once again thousands of U.S. soldiers and hundreds of thousands of innocent civilians died before we began our withdrawal.

So, where did this type of thinking come from? Certainly not from the public school and state university sector, not from the students who actually ended up fighting the war. Rather, it came from the unreal world of "bubble" education, a segment of our society that apparently lost contact with the real world a long time ago. This syndrome, which has been labeled the "bubble mentality," is not unique to the United States. The same progression played out in France before the French Revolution, in Russia before the Russian Revolution, in England before that country lost its empire. Historically, it has occurred when members of an elite cast who are sheltered from the real world during their formative years move into positions of power as a self-reinforcing clique and begin making disastrous decisions.

Is there a way to combat this mentality, to stop it before more damage is done to the U.S. economy, the U.S.'s image, the U.S.'s self-respect? Changing the characteristics of the private education system would be nearly impossible because the essence of that system is provision of a protected environment where those students whose families are able to afford it received more individual attention from well-educated instructors. This is a reasonable objective, until one takes into account the shortcomings we have been talking about and their consequences. The only suggestion that makes sense, thus far, has been to get rid of the bubble world entirely, and that would be extremely difficult to do.

11.3 Increased Government Involvement and Funding

Returning to our study of changes that occurred in the U.S. education system, from the 1950s on, things grew increasingly muddled. Following World War II, the United States was not able to relax. Instead, it became immediately involved in an arms race with the Soviet Union. The need for the United States was to produce a steady stream of scientists in a wide range of fields. At the same time, the nation needed to deal somehow with the thousands of servicemen and women returning home with the expectation of finding the employment needed to support themselves and their families.

The academic community benefitted from the necessary involvement of government in finding solutions to those problems. Large amounts of government funding became available for building science programs at all educational levels and for scientific research. Also, financial aid was made available to returning servicemen and women through the previously mentioned GI Bill of Rights. In 1945, over one million veterans took advantage of this benefit, immediately doubling the nation's college population. Eventually, over seven million veterans made use of the program before entering the workforce, helping to swell the middle class (Spring, p. 341).

Concerning the channeling of intelligent students into professions critical to national defense, in 1950, the National Science Foundation (NSF) was created to address this challenge. Part of the solution it developed was to amend the *Selective Service*

Act passed by Congress during World War II. The original act made every male eligible for the draft. The amendment said that if high school graduates didn't want to go into the military, an acceptable alternative was to continue with their education. Also, if while in college they gained expertise in an area critical to national defense and if, following graduation they found a job in that area, they could again avoid the draft.

As government involvement in the education sector expanded, ultra-conservatives, the right-wing Republicans who traditionally were against it taking part in shaping the academic process, grew increasingly perturbed. Eventually, they began claiming that the government, especially the public education system, had been infiltrated by Communists who wanted to destroy the U.S. democracy. In truth, there were probably some serious Communists teaching classes, as there are even today. Quite likely they did influence some students, or at least encourage them to take into consideration other perspectives. As history proves, however, their efforts exerted little influence on education theory, though right-wing radicals went after them, caught up in the anti-Communism frenzy of the day. The radical conservative fringe formed organizations such as Allen Zoll's National Council for American Education to focus attention on the dangers to our democracy resulting from what was going on in public schools. These organizations distributed pamphlets with titles such as *The Commies Are After Your Kids* and wrote articles. Textbooks that portrayed our enemies as anything but evil were sometimes banned by schools; public libraries were sometimes purged of materials suspected to be seditious (Spring, p. 395).

11.4 Academia's Failings in Terms of the U.S.'s Ability to Compete Globally

Meanwhile, a more legitimate charge that primary and secondary schools were watering down their curriculum too much was also being leveled by the conservative camp. The event that more than any other showed the seriousness of the situation was the Soviet Union's launching of Spudnik I in 1957. This startling wake-up call proved emphatically how far the United States had lagged behind in terms of the sciences. The conservatives used it to support their argument that the country needed to return to the basics—reading, spelling, grammar, and mathematics. They pushed for more emphasis on sciences. The conservatives pointed to the fact that while the United States seemed to be degrading public school curriculum to improve the success rate of slower students, the Europeans, Russians, and Japanese, our major competitors, were adding to it so that high school graduates in those countries had reached levels in most subjects roughly equivalent to that of college sophomores in the United States. Their mantra was basically "Forget about defining and meeting the needs of each individual. Focus on the basics, on making sure that students are given the opportunity to excel at the basics. Also, instead of watering the curriculum down, make it more challenging."

This conservatives' perspective was more global. What they worried about was their country's standing in the world. The United States was falling behind in the realm of education, especially in the sciences, and that was dangerous. At the same time, the Federal Government, blaming the NEA for this decline in the public education system, for the fact that the United States was falling behind countries it competed with economically, used this shortcoming as a rational for becoming increasingly involved in the formulation of national education policy.

11.5 The Students Get Involved

Conservatives and government officials, however, were not the only ones upset by what was going on in the education system and in society as a whole at this point in U.S. history.

Our founding fathers had believed that students should be the active participants in civic affairs as part of their education. During the 1960s and 1970s, their wish was finally honored. The social turmoil of the 1960s, bred by the Vietnam War, unrest amongst minorities, and the beginning of the drug culture, spawned protests on college campuses where rallies, the occupation of buildings, and class boycotts were organized by students. The movement turned violent at Kent State University in 1970 when National Guardsmen opened fire on protesters, killing four.

Reacting to the growing disillusionment of the young who were rebelling at the prospect of being sent to Vietnam to die in a war that made no sense to them, at the shooting of students who dared to speak out and act out, at the ongoing racism that still frequently turned violent, the Federal Government was forced to act. In an attempt to quell college student discontent, President Nixon (1969–1974) instituted a Career Education Program. The administration believed the underlying cause of this discontent to be that the education students were receiving did not lead to career opportunities. This logic was obviously a total conservative "spin" of the situation. Students and minorities were asking for more of a voice in society, for more freedom in making life choices. The right wing spun this to mean that they wanted to improve their chances of finding good jobs so that they could fit more easily into the status quo. At the same time the administration pushed this traditional conservative logic President Nixon was quietly cutting the education budget, citing as his reason for doing so the lack of evidence that the monies already spent had resulted in positive social change (Spring, p. 389).

One of the good things that did come out of the Nixon administrations' disconnect with reality was increased support for community colleges where the concept of "career education" actually fit. These two-year academic programs, indeed, met the needs of high school graduates who wanted to acquire training that would allow them to enter the job market immediately—as skilled practitioners, secretaries, computer operators, dental hygienists, mechanics, and so on.

11.6 Those Who Are Dissatisfied Strike Out on Their Own

The public school system, in the meantime, continued to experience difficulties. Complaints arose during the late 1960s and early 1970s that grade schools and high schools had grown too large and impersonal, doing little to address the needs of individual students. Obviously, changes were needed. But first, the Department of Education decided, some standard, some means of measuring where the system stood at a specific point in time and whether the situation began to improve or deteriorate as more time passed needed to be introduced. The buzzword became "accountability," and it led to a call for "competency testing," not only for students, but for teachers as well. Students had to demonstrate a certain level of comprehension in each subject to graduate. Teachers were required to demonstrate a level of comprehension in their area(s) of expertise to keep their teaching certificate.

Objections to this approach arose immediately. Who should have input concerning the content of the student tests? Was the concept of such a test, in itself, biased against underprivileged students or students representing cultures different from that of the writers? Would teachers begin teaching "to the test," leaving out other important things that should be covered? Was the testing process worth the cost when so many other things critical to a viable education system lacked funding?

Many of those dedicated to improving educational opportunities did not wait for the public school system to catch up. Instead they began designing and creating their own models, ones possessing the desired characteristics. Such home-grown institutions were called "alternative schools" and were usually smaller, community-supported affairs. During this period, some 5000 such schools were started. According to Terrance Deal and Robert Nolan in their article, "Alternative Schools: A Conceptual Map," these institutions were built around a set of themes, including:

1. A student's curriculum should be based on individual needs and experiences.
2. Teachers should function mainly as advisors to student efforts.
3. The school should function as a community.
4. Students should learn actively, by doing, rather than passively, though "chalk and talk."
5. As wide a range of learning resources as possible should be brought into play, with emphasis on those found in the community at large.
6. The skills students bring to class as well as those picked up in class should be viewed as vehicles for learning rather than accomplishments in themselves.
7. Student input should be considered as an important factor when making important decisions.
8. Continuing emphasis should be placed on nurturing the individual potential of both students and teachers (Button, p. 304).

Some alternative schools even went so far as to allow students to design their own curriculum. A major problem arose, however, with poorer students who suffered from the absence of a structured approach, who lacked the socialization experience and self-discipline required to put together their own learning process. Other problems with this approach included the number of highly trained teachers it necessitated and the number of schools the concept would require nationally if class size were to be manageable. Adam Smith once said that his contribution—modern day laissez faire economics—would work "...(only) in a perfect world." The same could probably be said for the alternative school concept, a very enlightened, compassionate approach, ideal for "a perfect world," but doomed to failure except in small, carefully cultivated pockets because of the amount of individual attention required.

As a result of their inability to spread into the mainstream, most alternative school ventures faded. One of the few that survived has been the better thought out Montessori Method developed by Italian physician Maria Montessori who opened her first school in 1907. Evidence of her approach's effectiveness and popularity rests in the fact that some 20,000 schools based on her work are currently in operation all over the world. Dr. Montessori incorporated many of the concepts that progressive educators in this country are currently talking about. Classes were mixed in terms of age, the most common mixture including children 2½ or 3 to 6 years old, though others have applied her techniques to groups including students up to the age of 18. Emphasis was on allowing independence, allowing students a large degree of freedom in the choice and conduct of activities, the child's psychological development being one of the school's primary consideration.

Children in modern-day Montessori classes are allowed to choose from a prescribed range of activities. After making their choice, they are allowed uninterrupted blocks of work time, achieving most of their learning by working directly with materials rather than through instruction. They learn by doing rather than by listening; they learn through working with their hands, through actual involvement in figuring out what needs to be accomplished, in figuring out how to solve the problem, which makes sense because, as we all know, learning by being told how to do something is a lot different from learning by doing it. The best coach in the world can explain to you how to shoot a basketball and get it into the hoop, but until you actually take a few shots (a few hundred?) you're not going to truly understand the process, the necessary flow.

The teacher in the Montessori system is more so a facilitator than a boss, not telling students what to do and how to do it, what to learn and how to remember it, but encouraging students to figure these things out by themselves, asking a lot of questions rather than giving answers. One of the key to the success of this approach is, again, the amount of individual attention given to students. The teacher–student ratio in these schools is much lower than that found in public schools.

The Montessori approach at the primary level is probably the best example of what humanists from Comenius on down, of what the human relations philosophy of education has advocated being successfully put into practice. The major challenge, once again, is how to provide individual students on a nation-wide or a world-wide basis with the required attention.

Chapter 12

Education in the United States during the Late 1900s

12.1 The Mechanistic Faction Refuses to Budge

The level of turmoil in the U.S. education system increased during the late 1900s. Competing factions continued to argue their viewpoint. New factions with new viewpoints materialized. One group that continued to voice its opinion in the strongest possible terms was the business community that wanted, as it had always wanted, schools to give students the skills necessary to find jobs and to contribute economically. Representatives of the business community wanted to shape curriculum according to the immediate needs of local companies and to deliver the same curriculum to everyone as a means of sorting the student population so that portions of it could be fitted comfortably into appropriate levels of the employee hierarchy.

They called for the development of accurate methods for measuring and comparing the achievement of students, including standardized curriculum, class grading systems based on test scores, and a comprehensive national testing system that allowed comparison on a state level. They wanted to do away with bilingual, multi-cultural courses and programs and get back to the Anglo-Protestant tradition of education. They wanted community education systems and curriculum to be controlled by professional managers rather than by local school boards. They wanted school administrators to be held accountable, to be judged by student performance on standardized achievement tests delivered annually and compared. "Standardization," "efficiency," "cost-effectiveness," "accountability," and "testing" were the most popular buzzwords in this group.

The business community's educational philosophy was supported by the work of B. F. Skinner, a psychologist who conducted studies concerning "behavioral engineering." This, in the scholastic arena, meant studies in the best way to shape and deliver course materials. Keep it simple; keep it on track; student progress should be orchestrated by experts; the input of students and other stakeholders should be gained through surveys. Skinner advocated testing to discover student deficiencies, then designing courses to cover these deficiencies, using reinforcement through repetition and reward to encourage students to learn what they needed to learn. Skinner believed that democracy—freedom of choice and expression—in both the classroom and in society hindered progress. To him, freedom was achieved when students were able to do the things they had been programmed to do without interference. No choice should be involved. As many of life's decisions as possible should be made according to the way one had been programmed by the education sector.

Conservatives, in their call for public school students to be programmed the same way employees had been programmed using Frederick Taylor's Scientific Management techniques, were mirroring the mindset made popular during the early Industrial Revolution. During that period, workers were treated basically as slaves, the definition of a "slave" in this instance being a worker who had to do what the owner demanded if he or she wanted to survive. The emphasis during Skinner's more modern research, however, was slightly different. The emphasis now was on turning workers into programmable robots. You were programmed to automatically do what you are told to do, to learn what you are told to learn without question or emotional response.

12.2 The Modern-Day Problem with the Mechanistic Argument

The problem, however, with this more modern approach was that while it wasn't slavery, it still failed to produce the desired results. The economic culture had changed radically since the Industrial Revolution, passing through several phases. Initially, it had been the industrialist with access to the most wealth who prevailed. J. P. Morgan, for example, at one point controlled a large part of the U.S. economy through his network of banks. When greater amounts of capital became accessible to those beginning and running businesses, it was the industrialist with the most advanced technology who succeeded. Henry Ford's moving assembly line, for example, gave him an advantage that lasted for several decades. Next came the information age. Companies that could generate or obtain access to the most useful information gained the advantage. This advantage, however, dissolved with rapid advances in computer technology, with rapid improvement in the way data could be collected, stored, manipulated, and turned into useful information.

Finally, creativity took the center stage. Computers and robots took over the grunt work, the manual jobs, and the jobs that required routine manipulation of data, so that what remained was planning, design, development of new products and businesses, and the improvement of processes important to production. The involved ability to think creatively, that is to come up with new ideas and approaches, could not be programmed into students through Taylor's and Skinner's methods, through the encouragement of step-by-step memorization coupled with reinforcement. Creativity required the ability, once the basics were in place, to charge off intellectually in untried directions and to put the pieces together in ways never before attempted. While the business community began to understand this shift in emphasis, the educational community lagged and was reticent to pay attention. The conservative group, still powerful, with its focus still on control, continued trying to force the educational community to more in the wrong direction, continued trying to force it to meet the needs of an industrial culture whose time had passed.

12.3 The Human Relations School Types Continue Chipping Away

The second major faction that continued to voice its viewpoint included those who wanted to focus on the development of individual student potential. This group sought to allow students a major say in picking their course of study. At the same time, it continued seeking ways to design classroom activities according to the beliefs of Rousseau, Piaget, Dewey, Montessori, and other education theorists who believed that students should play a major role in shaping the way they learned.

One approach introduced was the "open classroom." Rather than rows of desks with the teacher at the front delivering the lesson, the room was divided into learning stations between which students moved based on their interests and their progress in the different subject areas offered. The concept was tried, but did not survive for long owing largely to logistical difficulties. Whom do you move, when, and where? How do you keep track of individual progress in the different subject areas? And, again, how does the teacher satisfy the needs of both the average student and the very smart student who completes all the assignments covered at that grade level in the first week?

The third faction to develop a presence was the teachers who had finally decided to organize in order to give weight to their calls for decent wages, respect, a voice in curriculum, and policy matters. The National Education Association (NEA), discussed in earlier chapters, was dominated by administrators until the early 1960s. Its main role was to negotiate policy with school boards and the government. The American Federation of Teachers (AFT), formed in 1916, was run by teachers and offered a more radical approach to negotiation. Its members were unionized. The AFT originally had a no-strike policy. In 1960, however, after the Buffalo teachers struck on their own and their action was repeated by independent teachers' unions across the country, a New York affiliate of the AFT went on strike, thus establishing a more militant approach for the organization in its negotiations.

The issues first addressed by the AFT had to do with improving the teachers' quality of working life. They included increased pay, sick pay, class loads, and the amount of time allowed for lunch. Eventually, emphasis shifted to policy, to improving the way in which the education system was structured, especially the way in which decisions affecting teachers were made.

Power in the NEA also eventually shifted from administrators to teachers. The organization then got involved in politics. One of the Democratic candidates supported was Jimmy Carter, a contender for the Presidency of the United States. In return for the organization's support, upon being elected, President Carter created, in 1979, the Department of Education, the new Secretary of Education joining his cabinet to represent the interests of the educational sector.

Conservatives, who now shaped the perspective of the Republican Party, fought back. Upon regaining political power with the election of President Reagan (1981–1989), they tried to shut down the Department of Education, opposed bilingual education, and tried to amend the U.S. Constitution to give the growing number of private schools access to federal funds. They also tried to bring prayer back into the classroom. In 1962 and 1963, the Supreme Court had passed down a decision, based on First Amendment Rights, that holding prayer sessions in a school was unconstitutional owing to the need to separate church and state. The Republicans wanted to overturn this ruling.

12.4 Government Efforts to Make School Systems Accountable

In the 1970s, some states had, on their own, begun looking for ways to make schools academically accountable by setting a standard of proficiency that all students had to meet. This was called the "minimum competency" approach. Tests were administered at the end of each year. Students had to earn the required score in order to demonstrate their competency so that they could move onto the next grade level. Obviously, in modern times, with the greater range of challenges that now existed, it had become necessary to spell academic requirements out in more detail. The new, more fully thought-out policy that emerged was called "standards-based reform." It included three steps. First, the academic standards that students had to meet would be defined. Second, a means of measuring student progress toward these standards would be established. Third, schools would in some way be held accountable for demonstrating the progress of their students (Hanushek and Raymond, pp. 311–312).

In 1983, then Secretary of Education, T. H. Bell, created the National Commission on Excellence in Education to study the U.S. public education system and its shortcomings. The commission published *A Nation at Risk: The Imperative for*

Educational Reform, a report that, for the first time, looked at the system as a whole, framing it as a player on the world stage, warning that our public education system was falling behind, was not producing the caliber of student being produced in other countries and that, as a result, we were losing ground in the global economic race. It said that the minimum competency approach was not good enough, that we should switch to an input-focused approach that raised the bar, that set high expectations rather than just minimal ones. It said that not enough homework was being assigned, that teachers were poorly trained, emphasis in their education placed on pedagogy rather than on gaining the appropriate level of expertise in subject matter. It said that textbooks were being "dummied down," and that too much time was being spent on electives and on extra-curricular activities. The Commission recommended that high schools require "four years of English, three of science, three of social studies, one semester of computer science, and two of language for college-bound students." It said that more resources should be made available to public school systems in order to support these new requirements (Button, p. 314).

In 1987, The Carnegie Forum on Education and the Economy released *A Nation Prepared: Teachers for the Twenty-First Century,* a report generated in an attempt to give the profession of teaching more appeal. It proposed raising teacher's salaries. It also recommended that public school teachers become promotable. While the college and university system had the ranks of instructor, associate professor, assistant professor, and full professor, the only way public school teachers could gain anything similar to a promotion was to go into administration. The report suggested that they should start as "interns," progress to "residents," then, after at least 10 years of experience to "lead teachers" responsible for mentoring interns, for helping develop curriculum, for helping design and deliver teacher education programs. A salary increase, of course, would accompany each promotion.

12.5 Developing Statewide Achievement Standards and Work–Study Programs

By the mid-1990s, nearly every state had developed achievement standards and put them into place; nearly every state was testing students to see if students met these standards. Not all states, however, were putting into place a means of holding schools accountable for student progress. One of the major reasons they were reticent to include the accountability piece was that it changed the rules. Before, with the minimum competency and input-focused approaches, students were the ones held accountable. Now, the Federal Government wanted to hold states accountable, to reward those that performed well; to find some way to encourage those that did not. The name given to this approach was "consequential accountability" and by the end of the twentieth century, almost all states were on board with it.

President Ronald Reagan (1981–1989), a Republican, had campaigned to allow prayer in public schools and to provide government funds for private schools. His major emphasis, however, had again been on getting the business community more involved in improving the education system. Companies were encouraged to adopt a local school. The individual companies signed pacts saying that if the school would offer curriculum designed to meet the company's needs, the company, in turn, would give graduates preference when hiring. The Reagan administration also worked to shift responsibility in terms of both setting policy and providing funding from the national level to the state level.

George H. W. Bush (1989–1993), the next President, also a Republican, continued to encourage the alliance between business and education. His education goals included establishment of the privately funded, nonprofit New American School Development Corporation, the corporation's mission being to establish model schools across the nation from which local schools could learn. His goals included development of national education standards, development of national achievement testing, and encouragement of education choice. President Bush's program, which focused on preparing students for the workplace, was called Goals 2000.

The next U.S. President, Bill Clinton (1993–2001), a Democrat, supported the Goals 2000 program and expanded it to include preschool education for children, especially the underprivileged, as well as continuing education for adults. President Clinton also delivered the *School-to-Work Opportunities Act* creating programs that combined school-based and workplace-based learning. Students spent part of their traditional school time in paid workforce positions where they learned a trade.

Despite the continuing efforts of conservative politicians to diminish its role during this period, the Federal Government became increasingly involved in the education sector. In 1994, the *Improving America's Schools Act*, a revision of the President Johnson's *1965 Elementary and Secondary Education Act*, was passed. It mandated, by law, the use of state assessment tools to measure student progress toward state-defined standards so that those schools not performing well could be put on a list for "corrective action." Schools in this category faced an escalating series of interventions beginning with students being allowed to change schools or to receive tutoring at the expense of the school. The next requirement, following six years of continuous failure to make the required progress, was a restructuring plan that might include closing, reorganizing and reopening the school, replacing staff not doing a good job, allowing the state to take over, allowing a private management company to take over, or "any other restructuring of the school's governance designed to produce major reform" (U.S. Department of Education, "The Improvement of America's Schools Act of 1994").

Little such corrective action, however, actually occurred. For one thing, the states were still defining their standards individually and could downgrade them at will if students weren't doing well enough. For another thing, the federal government failed to put into place a vehicle to adequately monitor whether or not states were doing what was required.

12.6 Three Movements That Made a Difference

In the early 1990, three other movements were occurring in the education sector, these at the state level, which produced more far-reaching consequences than most previous efforts by U.S. Presidents or by the Department of Education. The involved changes began with a growing number of states allowing "freedom of choice," which meant that students were not required to attend the public school in their district but could choose to go elsewhere. The purpose of this decision was to allow students to seek a better education. Traditionally, the amount of funding districts received from the state depended on the tax monies collected in that district. As a result, schools in poorer districts were not funded as well and could not provide the same level of education as schools in wealthier districts.

The next movement that came along was "privatization." Private companies were asked to administer public schools and public school districts. Their main goal was to manage resources more efficiently, and to cut down on bureaucratic waste. Their level of reward was based on meeting goals set by the local school board or business community.

The third movement, the third leg of the stool, was the advent of "charter schools." States allowed companies, teachers, parents, or community groups to petition the local school board or the appropriate agency for the funds necessary to start a public school with a specific focus or to create a focused program in an existing school. Charter schools, for the most part, administered themselves. They were left alone so long as they continued to abide by the charter they had agreed to with the state. They did not have to follow the dictates of the local school board. Like magnet schools, they could cater to a segment of the student population interested in focusing on one subject area—say, theater or physics or industrial arts. They could also cater to individual populations such as Afro-Americans, Native Americans, Orthodox Jews, or the deeply religious Christians.

Obviously, the three movements fed into each other. Once freedom of school choice was established privatization became an attractive alternative as a means of making a school more appealing to potential students. The concept of privatization also encouraged those who wanted to start a charter school to take the chance, knowing they could get help in running it.

But the charter school concept, while coming closer to meeting individual needs and those of groups defined by their differences, like the magnet school concept developed during the 1960s obviously ran contrary to the traditional role assigned by our founding fathers to the public school system, to the role of providing the comprehensive education and the broad rather than focused perspective that one gained by being given access to a wide variety of both academic and social experiences.

Also, during this period, conservative elements of the Republican Party reiterated once again in a 1994 document, *Contract with America*, their desire to reduce tax-supported government expenditures. In terms of education, the *Contract with America* called for, among other things, cutting aid for disadvantaged students, for bilingual education, for school lunches, for charter schools, for President Clinton's school-to-work programs, and for the funding of the first President Bush's national standards program. The document said that emphasis should shift from the education system to the family; that parents, rather than "experts" should take the lead in making decisions concerning education for their children, and that government should stay out of such decisions.

Chapter 13

Education in the United States during the Early 2000s

13.1 No Child Left Behind (NCLB) and the Ensuing Confusion

In 2005, President George W. Bush (2001–2009) amended President Johnson's *Elementary and Secondary Education Act* once again, giving us *No Child Left Behind* (NCLB), an approach greatly expanding the influences of Federal and State governments in terms of student testing and the measurement of teacher proficiency. The program's goal was that every student would be proficient in math and reading at his or her grade level according to his or her state's standard by the year 2014. If schools receiving federal aid fell behind, their funding would be cut.

One of the cornerstones of the program was the adoption of previously mentioned "consequential accountability" as a national objective. This move strengthened the overall accountability requirement. At the same time, however, the NLBC amendment allowed states to continue developing their own standards and their own means of assessment. One might suspect that when federal funding was tied to achievement of these standards, states would be tempted to set them low. Also, because states were allowed to set their own standards, a hodge-podge existed, making the standards difficult to interpret and, as has been said, the results of testing difficult to compare. (*The Policy and Politics of Rewriting the Nation's Main Education Law*, pp. 45–46.)

In reaction to this apparent confusion at the federal level, some of the individual states once again stepped in, over 40 of them deciding to adopt "Common Core Content Standards." The question was, however, whether or not they could reach agreement on the individual standards in the common core? Doing so would produce another step toward leveling the playing field, toward allowing a more accurate interpretation of the academic accomplishment of individual students and of individual schools. But was it possible?

Another approach that was suggested, one that would be complimentary to the Common Core Standards approach, was to create a tiered set of standards. The base "proficient" level would hearken back to the "minimum competency" level of original efforts to make sense of academic progress. This level would be tied to the quest for federal funding and to the school's efforts to escape intervention. Besides that, however, schools would add an "advanced" level for students desiring more challenging curricula. The achievements of students in the advanced subjects, however, would not be taken into account when measuring progress toward the year 2014 goal of total school proficiency in math and reading. Only the progress of these students in traditional classes would be taken into account. In this way, by defining two levels, while the requirements of NCLB were being met, more attention was being paid at the same time to the full development of individual potential.

A second serious problem with NCLB was that schools were responsible for setting up the actual student testing procedure and for submitting test results upon which conse-quential accountability decisions depended. Schools found ways to discourage weaker students from taking the test. Some went so far as to place these students in special educa-tion classes that would exempt them from the testing. Some excused weaker students from school on the day of the test or gave them assignments that keep them busy while their class-mates took the test.

When President Barack Obama's (2008–till date) administra-tion came into office, it recognized these weaknesses of the NCLB model and introduced the latest *Reauthorization of the Elementary and Secondary Education Act* in an attempt to remedy them. This reauthorization was named, *A Blueprint for Reform* and stressed: (1) Improving teacher and princi-pal effectiveness; (2) Providing information to families to help them evaluate and improve their children's schools; (3) Implementing college-ready and career-ready standards; and (4) Improving student learning and achievement in America's lowest-performing schools by providing intensive support and effective interventions.

In terms of the NCLB weakness concerning individualized state standards, the *Blueprint for Reform* proposed replacing them with one national set of standards against which the progress of all students in all states would be measured. An alternative would be for individual states to develop an indi-vidual set of standards with the help of their local state univer-sity system.

13.2 The Advent of the Student Aptitude Test

The issue of setting standards was further complicated by the existence of another testing and comparison system for stu-dents, this one oriented only toward those wanting to attend college. The system was introduced in 1901 when the first College Board Test was administered, mainly to private school students. The subjects covered included English, French, German, Latin, Greek, history, mathematics, chemistry, and physics. In 1926, the SAT (Student Aptitude Test) was introduced and eventually replaced the College Board Test. The SAT required 3 hours and 45 minutes and included questions on the subjects originally taught by our school system—mathematics, writing, and critical reading. In terms of mathematics, the areas covered included numbers and operations, algebra and functions, statistics, probability, and data analysis. In terms of writing, the areas covered included grammar and diction. Critical reading included "sentence-level reading." In 1957, a competitor to the SAT, the American College Testing (ACT) system became popular in middle-America schools. The test took approximately the same amount of time to complete as the SAT. It included English, mathematics, reading, science, reasoning, and, as an option, writing.

13.3 Why a Universal Test Taken by All Students Is Necessary

There were, of course, those who opposed the use of such tests as a determinant of which colleges and universities individual students would gain admittance to. The front page of the August 27, 2011 edition of the *USA Today* newspaper carried an article entitled, *"Love It Or Hate It, The SAT Still Rules."* The article discussed reasons for opposing the SAT and ACT tests as a standard against which to measure the learning of students. The reasons presented included the belief that they favor "affluent white students, especially males;" that they discriminate against students from poor families because such families frequently cannot afford to pay for preparatory tutoring prior to the exam; that some schools spend class time preparing students for the test that should be spent on normal subjects.

Owing to these concerns and others, some colleges and universities are beginning to pay less attention to the involved scores and more attention to classroom achievement and extra-curricular activities when evaluating candidates. But support-ers agree with the article. Many think that, while improvement is obviously possible and desirable, such tests "still rule," that they are here to stay and must be here to stay. Supporters also believe that the scores earned on such tests should take pre-cedence over grades in determining the institutions of higher learning that individual students will be accepted by.

This opinion stems from a suspicion that grades are more easily corrupted than test scores and are frequently less indica-tive of true student potential. We have no universal standard to refer to when deciding who gets an "A." While such a stan-dard obviously does exist for the SAT/ACT, there is no such thing for high school grading systems, nothing that comes even close. The basis of such decisions differs from school to school, from teacher to teacher, in both the public and private sector, and is influenced by a wide range of variables.

The current emphasis on class rank is one such variable. It is pretty well accepted that the colleges and universities con-sidered the best academically look for applicants in the top 10% of their class grade-wise, relaxing that requirement for some schools, mostly private ones, which have an excellent reputation for academics. In the average public school, how-ever, this competition for the top 10% can include a range of different groupings. It can include just students taking honors or advanced placement (AP) level courses. It can include those along with students in the college prep tract, which is not fair because the honors or AP course students frequently receive a grade boost. If students in honors or AP courses receive a "B" (worth three points in terms of grade point average), they are awarded four points instead. If they receive an "A" (4 points) they are awarded five points. One of the results of this arrangement is that the straight "A" college prep student who has decided not to take honors or AP level courses, no matter how intelligent, can end up well down in the pile.

Another approach to this competition is to include all students in the class ranking—those doing honors level work, those in college prep, those in the technical education tract, and even those in special education. The parents of the latter two groups feel that placing their children in a different category is a put-down, which is a reasonable argument.

The problem with this approach is that students in the technical education and special education sectors frequently earn "A"s, possibly because teachers know that most of them are not planning to pursue further formal education and, therefore, the major purpose of grades, again, is to teach discipline and to build self-esteem. As a result of this system, we find a thick layer of students around the 4.0 level in the class ranking. Students in the straight college prep tract, because their course work is more difficult, and also students taking honors or AP courses because they are often doing college level work, might end up with less than 4.0, or might end up in only the top 20% or even the top 30% of their class.

13.4 Grades Don't Tell the Story

This brings us to the second point. The purpose of education, as has been said by a steady stream of thinkers throughout history, is to help students discover and develop their potential to the fullest possible extent. Almost all colleges and universities say they look for students willing to challenge themselves, to take the difficult courses. The recruiting system of these institutions, however, with its focus on class ranking does not encourage this. Because competition is so fierce for the top-level schools—some receive as many as 30,000 applications for 2000 or 3000 slots—students interested in attending them are forced to focus on grades rather than on learning as much as possible; they are forced to "play the game," to define that combination of honors or AP courses and normal college prep courses that will give them the highest average. If students are strong in mathematics, for example, but not English or history, they will sign up for the advanced mathematics and physical sciences courses but only for college prep English and history, rather than challenging themselves in these subjects and possibly learning more in the advanced classes.

Another trick is to take gut electives graded pass–fail. The reason for doing so is that the highest grade one can receive in an elective is usually a 4.0. Even if one receives an "A," therefore, it will drag an above 4.0 average down. "Gut" electives, because they are pass–fail, will not do so, even though the student might have no interest in what is being taught.

A third serious issue that arises when grades are the major consideration for college admission is that teachers, increasingly, become targets. The more intense the competition for class ranking, the greater the number of irate parents the teacher has to deal with who want Johnny to attend Duke, who want to know why Johnny didn't receive an "A" when he worked so hard for one and needed one? Such pressure affects both the teacher's attitude and performance.

The fourth factor that has to be taken into account is teacher bias. There are two types of such bias. The first has been called "general bias." It concerns how hard teachers decide to make their courses. This can vary greatly. A tremendous amount of work can be required in one section and very little in another section of the same course, depending on whom the teachers are. The amount of work required obviously influences the grade received and, eventually, class ranking.

The second type of teacher bias has been called "personal bias." We all have personal biases; it is natural. However, in the academic world, such biases can and do affect grades and class ranking. A male teacher who doubles as a coach may favor athletes and give them a break. A female teacher might favor the girls in her class. Or the preferential treatment might be based on attitude, or on appearance. Though teachers usually try to get beyond them, such biases are inevitable and can make a difference in class ranking.

Making some form of universal testing, administered either as part of secondary school courses or at the end of secondary school, the primary determinant for college admission is one way to resolve these problems. This approach does two things. First, as is frequently noted, it levels the playing field; gives everyone an equal opportunity if they are properly prepared. Second, and not as frequently noted but much more important, it encourages students to focus on learning as much as possible in secondary school, rather than on achieving the highest possible grade point average.

Ranking systems based on grades when there is no standardization inevitably give some groups the advantage. As a result, such systems provide colleges and universities with a skewed perspective concerning student potential. There is no way they cannot. If the objective, therefore, is to identify students with the most academic potential from across the nation, the best alternative is obviously to have them all take the same test.

Concerning the previously mentioned concerns with such tests, the solution is not to change the test, not to make it more comfortable for individualized populations of students. No matter what is done, somebody will lose out unless we go through the exercise of identifying the whole range of possible groupings and developing a "comfortable" test for each grouping, this being a project without end. Also, a great number of sensitive questions would need to be answered in this instance including, "Who makes up the test and how are socio-economic and cultural biases avoided?" "How can a test address a student's full range of abilities and intelligences and, if it cannot, where should the focus be?"

13.5 No Perfect Solution, But…

There is obviously no perfect answer to this challenge; there never will be. Probably the best that teachers can do is to discover which major subjects the colleges and universities believe secondary school students need education in and to help design the test to make sure that they are properly prepared. An advantage of this approach is the student's realization that scores earned on a comprehensive, standardized exam taken at the end of secondary school will be the prime determinant of where he or she attends college. This realization, as has been said, will encourage students to focus more so on learning than on grades. Earning all "A"s will not mean as much. Grades should still be a factor, they are the other side of the coin, but they will no longer be as important. In this instance, if a student has to choose between taking a gut elective in order to maintain a high grade point average and taking a tough elective in biology, the student's major field of interest, the choice will be much easier to make, the result much more beneficial in terms of the student's intellectual advancement.

In terms of teachers becoming targets, things will also change for the better. Instead of worrying mainly about Mary's or Johnny's grade on the history test, or about why it was a "B" instead of an "A," parents will worry about whether their children are learning what they are supposed to be learning. They will worry about whether or not the teacher is properly preparing and is presenting the material effectively. In the same edition of *USA Today* mentioned earlier, an editorial entitled, *"Principals Too Quick To Use 'Teacher Shortage' As An Excuse"* offered the percentage of public school teachers lacking a major or a minor in the subjects they taught to grade 9 through 12 students (1999–2000). For the subject of history, the figure was 58%; for English 24%; for science 20%; and for social studies 20%.

This, of course, means that the subject is usually taught straight from the book with very little elaboration. It also means the students don't learn as much. When grades and class ranking reign supreme, the question is too frequently, "Okay, we see that Mr. Straus is at a disadvantage, having no formal training in the subject. How do we work him to get an 'A'?" When learning as much as possible is the challenge, however, the question changes. It becomes, "How do we make sure that our teachers are qualified to teach what they are supposed to be teaching?" An entirely different emphasis emerges.

Finally, in terms of teacher bias, while Mr Bell or Ms Mahoney can use flexible criteria when marking papers or can give somebody a break when entering grades, he or she cannot legitimately favor certain students when disseminating information. The teacher cannot go around whispering what needs to be known into the ear of the chosen. Everyone attends the lectures; everyone receives the homework assignments; everyone works on the same problems; everyone has a chance to ask questions. The playing field, as we have said, is leveled when the focus is on learning in preparation for a final exam rather than on short-term grades.

The test we are talking about as the major determinant of college and university acceptance needs to be more comprehensive than either the SAT or the ACT. Its range needs to be expanded to cover all primary subjects—mathematics, English, history, and sciences other than math, foreign language, and geography. In order to do this effectively, the length of the testing period must also be extended, lasting several days instead of just hours.

13.6 European Nations Provide Models the United States Can Learn from

At this point, rather than reinventing the wheel, we need to ask if such an approach is already in place elsewhere. And, of course, it is. Historically, the United States, at least in its early days, modeled itself primarily on Europe. For example, our approach to economics, originally laissez faire or free enterprise, was a product of European thinking and was exported to the colonies. Democracy as a form of government was also the product not so much of our Continental Congress as it was of the drawing rooms of France and England, where the great minds of the era gathered to share ideas.

Education of the general public, the belief that providing every citizen with the opportunity to develop his or her intellectual potential would, in the long run, provide the greatest good for the nation as a whole, was also originally a European concept. The first nationally integrated public school system was developed in Europe. Countries such as France, Holland, Germany, Sweden, and Switzerland have been at it a lot longer than the United States, and, eventually, came to the conclusion that a comprehensive examination at the end of the secondary education period or, at least, some type of standardized measurement vehicle was the best alternative.

Perhaps, once again, we can learn from and build on European ideas and approaches. In France, for example, an exam called the Baccalaureate (Bac) is administered to graduates of secondary school. Everyone who wishes to enter one of the country's 77 universities must pass it. Two broad groupings of tests exist—the Bac General and the Bac Tecnnologique. The first, the Bac General, includes three categories—literature, economics, and sciences. The second, the Bac Technologique, includes tests in medical-social technologies, industrial technologies, laboratory technologies, and tertiare technologies. Scores from all the tests taken by a student in the chosen grouping are averaged. Universities frequently do not even bother to look at the course grades earned by individual students throughout their years of schooling.

Bac tests are standard throughout the nation. Several thousand questions must be answered. In some subjects, part of the test is oral. Essays are written. The test taker's name is concealed. Teachers are not allowed to grade tests completed by students in their own school. If students fail the Bac, receive an averaged score too low to be accepted by a university, they are allowed to make another attempt six months later. If they fail the second time as well, they must repeat their last year of school before trying again.

While no system, as has been said, is perfect, the French seem to prefer the Bac alternative to others. In the mid-1980s, a suggestion by the ruling political party that grades be given more importance precipitated massive student demonstrations.

Sweden has moved in the same direction as the United States, but with at least one critical difference. Traditionally, Swedish students interested in continuing onto a University have also taken a test, the Studenten, similar to the Bac. In the 1980s, however, policy was changed and the focus shifted to course grades. If a student's grades are high enough, the desired program in the desired university will accept that person without seeing Studenten test results. The government sets a grade average level based on the number of students graduating each year and the number of seats open at universities. A student whose grade point average lies above that level is accepted. If a student's grade point average does not lie above that level, a set of standardized tests similar to our SATs can be taken to improve chances. Finally, if the student does not do well enough either with grades or on the standardized tests but still wants to eventually attend a university, that person can find a job and earn credits toward acceptance based on years of work experience.

Do Swedes have to deal with the same problems found in the United States—an unleveled playing field due to different approaches to class ranking, a focus on grades rather than on learning, pressure on instructors, teacher bias? The answer is "no," or, at least, not to the same degree. Behind this difference lies the fact that Swedish schools have a standardized curriculum, and, more important, that they give nationally standardized tests in the different subjects. Class performance is also taken into account, but the standardized tests provide a valid basis for comparison and help level the playing field in terms of grades.

Switzerland, again, has a different approach. All students who graduate from the upper secondary school, roughly equivalent to U.S. grade 11 through sophomore year in college, are accepted by their chosen university in their chosen course of study. The only field where a competitive examination must be taken, owing to the current high level of demand, is medicine. Acceptance decisions in this last situation are based on examination scores.

The Swiss approach derives mainly from that country's ongoing efforts to make sure that all universities offer roughly the same quality of education. Once again, the playing field is leveled, but this time because "better" and "worse" universities do not exist and because everyone who graduates from secondary school is guaranteed acceptance, thus eliminating the need for competition. Emphasis for the student is on learning as much as possible; it is on doing one's best in order to achieve the grade point average necessary to graduate.

In summary, four different approaches, those of the United States, France, Sweden, Switzerland, have been explored. The last three depend on standardization—standardization of a comprehensive final exam, standardization of subject matter and testing during secondary school years, standardization of the quality of university education—in efforts to provide their young with the best educational opportunities, and in efforts to develop the potential of their young to the fullest possible extent.

In the United States, despite President Bush's and President Obama's efforts, we seem, currently, to be moving in the opposite direction, toward destandardization, toward more focus on grades and on class ranking when there is no way to ensure that the work done is comparable, when there is no way to ensure that we are comparing apples and apples while awarding class rank.

The United States seems reticent to standardize when it is an absolutely necessity if we want to shift the emphasis in our schools back toward learning. The alternative models are there. They have been tested and proven. It is time for us to take these models into serious consideration. It is time for us to learn once again from the greater experience of the European cultures that first helped shape U.S. society.

Chapter 14

Europe: Leading the Way or Behind?

14.1 Designing the Best Model

The debate in Europe does not focus as much on whether to cater to the individual student versus bringing the entire student population up to a specified level of learning as it does in the United States. Emphasis in Europe does not reside in the individual realm. Rather, the debate there focuses more so on how the education system should be shaped and where the emphasis for teachers should lie. Until recently, every European nation had its own model, pieced together through the centuries, mired in bureaucracy and outdated regulations, individualized, and difficult to challenge. Then, in 1996, in an attempt to draw these different models together and make sense of them in terms of the European education system as a whole, the Council of Europe, formed by the European Union (EU), an economic and political union of 27 European states, proposed a list of common values for all involved nations to subscribe to. The list included human dignity, fundamental freedoms, equitable growth, the rejection of violence, dialogue, and respect for others.

This list came to be known as the bedrock of the "European Dimension" and of the EU's efforts to make a whole of the continent's parts. It stressed democracy, pluralism, and interculturality, which, one might say, are modern-day substitutes for the battle cry of "liberty, equality, and fraternity" that drove the French Revolution during the late 1800s. The European Dimension became a common foundational piece of education systems across the continent. According to Roxanne Enache in her article *Building National Unity and Curriculum Uniqueness in the European Context,* the European Dimension "implies the manifestation of European consciousness (sharing the same values, respecting the same rights and freedoms, basing actions on the same philosophy, inspiring attitudes and behaviors of the same culture within initially different cultures)" (Enache, p. 18).

Education systems, in order to contribute to the integration across cultures desired by the EU, needed to include a political dimension that taught students how to participate effectively in a democracy; a legal dimension that taught them their rights and responsibilities; a cultural dimension that taught respect for those who were different; social and economic dimensions that taught the role of the economy in positive societal development; and a European dimension that familiarized students with the diversity found within the EU, that sold students on the value of the comprehensive whole that putting all the parts together built (Enache, p. 18). Concerning "positive societal development," it must be remembered, as was pointed out in Chapter 1, that Europe is not unfamiliar with the Development Ethic. Although it is just being discovered or rediscovered in the United States, where the growth ethic and the individualism that the growth ethic encourages still dominate, it had been "popping up" throughout European history as a major generator of improvement in all realms of society, calling for a cooperative effort, saying that cooperation is more productive.

While European nations have certainly gone through periods of self-centered aggrandizement—the continent's history of almost nonstop intercultural warfare provides ample proof of this, as does the excesses of the early Industrial Revolution—they continue to return to the development ethic as a guiding principle. So their desire to make the system as a whole more productive, rather than just the individuals being taught in that system, should not be unexpected.

Enache finishes with "Therefore, to be European means to get involved in solving common problems, to learn to cooperate and communicate, to participate in the civil life of the society" (Enache, p. 19). The EU's ultimate goal was to help unify member nations culturally by defining a set of common values and by encouraging movement toward a *federal* Europe, this concept first being introduced and encouraged in 1943 by Count Richard N. Coudenhove-Kalergi as a means of stopping European nations from tearing themselves and each other apart. In more modern times, the move toward federalization means standardization of electoral systems, manufacturing requirements, legal systems, healthcare systems, employment law, and education models; it means granting citizens of member nations the right to seek employment in other member nations.

At the same time, the EU has encouraged increasing degrees of standardization in these areas, however, it has also encouraged the spread of individual national cultures across traditional borders; it has given countries the chance to learn from each other and to incorporate what they find valuable from other societies.

One of the major impediments to progress in the EU's attempt to integrate the nations of Europe is the fear of losing national identity and the benefits that such identity provides. "If I become a European first, does that mean I have to sacrifice the traits and beliefs that make me British or French or German or Italian? Is the trade-off worth it? Can I gain the benefits of becoming a European while still retaining those of my native culture?" Efforts to ease these doubts are being introduced at the primary and secondary school levels where the previously mentioned European Dimension had been added to the curricula. The purpose of these efforts is to familiarize EU students with each other's cultures.

Research has shown that students who have traveled, who have spent time in foreign countries are more positive about the proposed integration (Convery and Kirstin, pp. 29–30). Therefore, the familiarization effort at primary and secondary levels includes adopting a "twin town" in another nation. Students communicate with students in these twin towns, share gifts, and even exchange visits. In some instances, the twin towns arrange short-term employment opportunities, maybe summer jobs, for older students. The Internet, of course, has also played a large role in such familiarization efforts, allowing students to go far beyond classroom exercises in establishing and maintaining contacts with their peers from other nations in the EU.

14.2 The Bologna Process' Focus on Standardization

One of the things critical to the success of Europe's education reform efforts has been the setting of standards. The EU has long since developed standards for manufactured goods. It is now in the process of doing so for education systems as well. Great Britain under Prime Minister Margaret Thatcher took the lead in this effort by requiring a more thorough evaluation of both student's and teacher's performances, their research proposals and results, by requiring a more thorough evaluation of what was being offered in terms of how it enhanced the public good.

Also, as part of its effort to standardize offerings, the European Commission has supported adoption of the Bologna Process, which organizes university-level learning into a "3-2-3" sequence. This means that students in European countries now spend three years in the undergraduate levels, two years at the master's degree level if one pursues a master's degree and three years at the PhD level, though many believe that the second year of master's level work should be considered part of PhD studies, in that the work being done frequently contributes to these studies, thus changing the progression to 3-1-4.

To meet the involved requirements, representatives of 29 countries met at The Lisbon Recognition Convention in 1997 where they agreed on a set of education credentials and a hierarchy of education levels at which the credentials would be awarded. In 1998, representatives of France, Germany, Italy, and Great Britain then met and signed the *Sorbonne Declaration* vowing to find ways to update the European system. The countries worked together to create a common degree structure that allowed students to move more freely between university-level schools in their own country and to those in other European countries. They also hoped this change would make their schools more attractive globally, an incentive for their efforts being the fact that in the late 1900s the United States had taken the lead in efforts to enroll foreign students in its universities.

The French government, as part of this effort, created EduFrance, a well-funded agency, given the task of recruiting 500,000 students mainly from Asia and South America (Charlier and Croche, p. 12). The French model suggested that students pay tuition fees to help support the universities attended, as is done in the United States and England, though not nearly as much as students in the United States pay.

The German system was also suffering from cost problems. Students felt no need to complete their studies, often taking long breaks to hold jobs or to do other things. This attitude generated extra costs for the universities and for the government. By formally adopting the Bologna Process' 3-2-3 architecture for undergraduate, master's, and PhD-level studies along with most of Europe, German universities encouraged students to finish their schooling in a shorter period of time so that they could take jobs commensurate with their now better qualifications, jobs that contributed more to the greater good. In order to attract increasing numbers of students from other countries, Germany began offering grants and encouraging foreign graduates to stay in the country for a year following completion of their course work to look for jobs.

Italy had not traditionally encouraged foreign students to study at its universities and, therefore, had not benefited from the additional income they provided. Other problems included students not completing their studies while spending a lot of time in not doing so and curricula not being adapted to the demands of the marketplace. The Bologna Process was again used as an excuse for reforming the Italian education system. More emphasis was placed on recruitment. An effort was also mounted to grant Italian universities more autonomy in designing their curricula.

The British, as a participant in the Bologna Process, encouraged policies that allowed greater flexibility in course and program design, that allowed the transfer of credits between universities, that encouraged the adoption of quality standards, that called for higher tuition fees based on the student's ability to pay, and that created deferred tuition payment mechanisms (Charlier and Crocke, p. 16). Concerning the 3-2-3 progression, England insisted on retaining its one-year master's-level degree program.

The Bologna Process is currently working to developing a university- and graduate-level education system that includes four types of public institutions. The most traditional is the university that awards undergraduate, master's, and PhD-level degrees, with research playing an important role. The second type includes institutes of applied sciences that specialize in the provision of occupation-oriented skills such as business, engineering, languages, tourism, social work, and the design of information systems, where students begin immediately to prepare for their chosen occupation. While those receiving their degree from institutes of applied sciences can move at the end of their undergraduate studies into master's degree-level programs at their home institution or transfer to a university for additional studies, most prefer to leave the education sector and find jobs. No doctoral-level programs are offered and no research is done. The third type of institution includes free-standing specialty institutions that offer mainly medical training and advanced degrees in the arts. The fourth type includes schools that provided a bridge between secondary school and university-level institutions. This type is similar to community colleges and junior colleges in the United States (Adelman, pp. 8–9).

14.3 The Bologna Process and Program Design

The Bologna Process has, at the same time, focused its efforts in four major areas of ongoing improvement. The first area is program design. European students spend more time than students in the United States at the secondary school level and cover more material, advancing to higher levels of comprehension in individual subjects. The average age of high school graduates in the United States is 17 to 18, whereas in Europe it ranges from 19 to 23. The previously discussed standard examinations are administered to all graduating students in a number of subjects. Admission to university-level institutions is not usually decided on a competitive basis. If students' scores are high enough, they can enter any school they wish. Variations to this approach, however, exist. In some instances, grade point averages are considered along with standard examination results; in other instances, labor market conditions are taken into consideration and caps set.

Once students gain admission to an undergraduate institution, however, acceptance into specific majors is competitive. If a student wants to remain in a specific school and the program he or she wishes to follow is full, that person might have to change to another major. Who gets into a program when not everybody who applies can do so is sometimes determined by differences in standard examination scores or by a combination of examination scores and grade point average, or sometimes by lottery.

University-level curriculum in European schools does not include the "general education courses" required by U.S. universities. Students begin studying immediately in their area of interest, which can be considered a drawback. Most of what the United States calls general education requirements, however, has been covered during the additional time spent in secondary school. Also, European university students are awarded a relatively large number of electives they can use in any way desired during their years of study.

This arrangement fits nicely with the 3-2-3 cycle that is becoming the international standard. Some argue that the U.S.'s 4-2-3 system gives students more study time, making up for the extra secondary school education required by the European system. When one looks more closely, however, this is not quite so. When Europeans talk about three years of undergraduate studies, they mean three years of full-time undergraduate study rather than three years of calendar time spent in school. Our four years of undergraduate work required to earn a degree include summer and Christmas breaks, three to four months of off-time each cycle that add up to close to a year so that, according to the numbers, students in the United States actually spend less study time at the university level than students in Europe.

Concerning the master's degree, a growing number of European students are making an effort during their undergraduate studies or taking time off between their undergraduate and graduate studies to find an internship in their field of interest, thus coming into their master's degree already possessing relevant knowledge and experience. The internship, in fact, is now being considered almost a prerequisite for acceptance into an increasing number of master's-level programs, just as a masters in one's chosen field is considered to be a prerequisite for finding a decent job.

14.4 The Bologna Process and Rewarding Student Accomplishment

The second area of focused improvement in the Bologna Process is development of a more standardized qualification frameworks, defining a way to evaluate and reward student accomplishment that makes sense, that is useful in terms of the education sector's role in society, and that will be respected by all nations. The qualification framework sets learning objectives as building blocks, where the required levels of learning are built upon these blocks, including the same general subject content in all participating countries. The purpose of this model is to create a "zone of mutual trust" where individual schools are willing to accept the academic achievements of a student from another country as valid for a specific level without forcing that student to repeat courses. Although the names for the various levels might differ in different countries, the content required remains roughly the same. The qualification frameworks are defined in terms of learning outcomes, the amount of challenge involved, the competencies developed, and student workload. The student's abilities are expected to increase and to expand at every level completed.

The Bologna Process continues to push for increased standardization in terms of qualification frameworks. At the same time, however, it realizes that total standardization, even if it were possible, would be a bad idea. Education is about learning what is necessary for one to function effectively in society; it is about learning what is necessary to make a contribution. Societies differ in many ways, these differences shaping their character and frequently their strength. Total standardization of the education system's qualification framework would eliminate the impact of many of these characteristics.

14.5 Strata of Qualifications Frameworks

Countries involved in the Bologna Process are working to develop three strata of qualifications frameworks. The first is the "global" strata affecting all participating nations. The requirements that have been agreed on thus far in this stratum include students demonstrating the defined level of learning at each reference point in each area of study before progressing onto the next level. The second requirement involves students understanding the value of what they have learned and how to use it in a positive manner. The third is gaining the ability at each level to use the increasingly sophisticated data and information presented in an effective manner. The fourth is to achieve a comprehensive, holistic understanding of what is being learned as well as of the complete range of stakeholders involved. The fifth is to gain support in terms of preparatory knowledge and the freedom from ignorance necessary to continue onto the next level.

The second stratum is "national." This is where the diverse characteristics of the countries involved help shape what is offered as well as how it is offered. Since the input and agreement of all the universities in a nation, say France, is required to define a qualification framework at this level, the process is taking much longer. The degree of focus on process versus content, the number of subject fields offered, the level of attention paid to the labor market when designing a school's offering, the national review process for what individual institutions have chosen to offer, all these things take time. Also, emphasis in the Bologna Process is more so on the harmonization of different universal and national systems than it is on their standardization. Emphasis is on shaping the approach to evaluation in individual nations so that schools in that nation can use the approach as a model, so that, ideally, it complements the approaches of other nations rather than conflicting with them to create the previously mentioned zone of trust, credentials earned in one country remaining valid when borders are crossed.

The third stratum is "institutional." University-level schools are expected to spell out what is taught to students at each level of study in each course. That they do this spelling out themselves helps maintain their autonomy. But, while accomplishing this task, those involved must keep in mind and shape their programs and courses to fit into the qualifications framework being generated at the national stratum level, which, in turn, must fit into the qualifications framework being generated at the global stratum level.

14.6 Shaping Curriculum through Tuning

This process at the program and course-shaping level is called *tuning*. The European Commission, its main mission being to help the EU unify European cultures through education, funded the involved effort and officially named it, Tuning Educational Structures in Europe. More than 100 universities joined, attempting initially to define "required general and subject-specific competencies in the areas of business, chemistry, education, the sciences, geology, history, mathematics, and physics" (Tomusk, p. 91).

The tuning process usually began with a survey of stakeholders to discover what they believed the general learning outcomes of a specific major should be. In terms of constantly improving knowledge, skills, and competencies, those who participated in the exercise included in the resultant list the ability of students to

- Demonstrate knowledge of the foundation and history of their major field.
- Demonstrate understanding of the overall structure of the discipline and the relationships both among its subfields and to other disciplines.

- Communicate the basic knowledge of the field (information, theories) in coherent ways and in appropriate media (oral, written, graphics, etc.).
- Place and interpret new information from the field in context.
- Demonstrate understanding and execution of the methods of critical analysis in the field.
- Execute discipline-related methods and techniques accurately.
- Demonstrate understanding of quality criteria for evaluating discipline-related research (Adelman, p. 35).

Then participants turned to the challenge of defining what the curriculum of each major needed to include in order to ensure these outcomes. When tuning was eventually applied at the individual course level, the exercise began by identifying what students should learn from that course. Next, the process listed the educational activities considered necessary to the desired learning. Next, it estimated the number of hours required to complete the involved activities. Finally, the process included a method of assessing the student's performance in that course.

Professors in the resultant system are required to decide how many hours students need to develop a sufficient understanding of each individual instruction point. This requirement forces them to evaluate their course offerings thoroughly, to decide what is most important, what is peripheral; to decide what should be core, what should be optional, and what should be replaced.

The major challenge faced during this process, of course, is coming up with an accurate estimate for the number of work hours required to complete individual educational activities, especially those pursued at home or, at least, outside the classroom or laboratory. Attempts have been made to do so through surveys of students who have completed the activity. Factors that influence such results, however, include whether students hold a job or not, their age, sex, home environment, previous education, and study habits. One way to address the variance found in such results would be to survey only top students, discovering the number of hours they dedicate to each activity, then to use these findings as a model.

Another key characteristic of the tuning system is that students are required to earn a certain number of credits at each level of their major. This prevents them from "stuffing," from earning a greater number of credits from lower, easier levels, avoiding the more demanding requirements of the upper levels.

14.7 Top-Down versus Bottom-Up Standardization

The overall purpose of tuning, again, is to define course parameters, rather than to identify exact requirements. Tuning has to balance academic autonomy with efforts to standardize, not an easy task. In the United States, a similar movement toward standardization of programs and curriculum is sputtering, owing largely to politics in that the two major parties describe the role of education in very different terms. The approach being used in the United States is also diametrically opposed to that taken in the EU. Instead of starting at the global or, in our case, national stratum, and creating an extremely generalized qualification frameworks, then working at the national level (which in the United States would be the state level) to identify learning requirement that incorporate national (state) characteristics for individual university-level institutions to meet while molding their programs and course content, the U.S. approach begins at the institutional level. The objective here is for all institutions to identify what they consider appropriate course content, and then to eventually bring these institutions and models together to delineate requirements for the state level.

While in Europe the standardization effort, therefore, is being built top-down, decisions being made first at the global level, then at the national level based partially on input from individual institutions; in the United States, an attempt is being made to build it bottom-up with individual institutions in individual states doing the initial work and providing the initial input. The weakness of this latter approach is obvious. Without a frame of reference at the state level to help shape ideas, the program and course design effort is going to take much longer to reach fruition, if it ever does. Our individualistic, "I'm going to do it my own way" attitude will once again become a major impediment to progress.

14.8 The Bologna Process and Transferability of Evaluation

The third major focus of the Bologna Process has to do with transferability of evaluation, with how best to evaluate student progress, with how to do so in a way that allows the transfer of recognized student credits to other schools both in the home nation and in other nations. Concerning student evaluation, the European system follows the dictates of the European Credit Transfer System (ECTS) introduced in the early 1990s to allow students in the ERASMUS Program who spent time studying in foreign universities to transfer the credits earned back to their home school. Currently, the system makes it possible for a degree or credits earned by anyone in any EU nation, be it the student's home nation or otherwise, to be honored in all EU nations. Eventually, this opportunity will be granted as well to nations outside Europe that adopt the Bologna Process.

14.9 The Bologna Process and the Social Dimension

A fourth focus has to do with the social dimension, by making education accessible to all populations. The EU movement believes strongly that educational opportunity makes possible economic opportunity, and that both these inputs are important to societal development. The Bologna Process in its efforts to enhance access to education is constructing "bridges." One such bridge is the development of a hierarchy of intermediate, short-term degrees that students can earn through bachelor-level studies; these degrees not requiring further course work. A second bridge is the addition of course schedules that attract part-time students, say students who, due to their job, can attend classes only at night, or those who want to attend classes during weekends. A third bridge is the awarding of credits toward the desired degree for a student's workplace experience.

A fourth bridge is the development of a diploma supplement that will accompany each diploma awarded and will outline the levels of knowledge and skill that individual students have actually achieved. The value of this addition is that while a diploma shows students' areas of completed study, the diploma supplement shows what they have learned in those areas and to what level that learning or skill building has progressed so that future employers as well as graduate programs applied to can gain a better idea of what the student has to offer.

Chapter 15

To Join or Not to Join? That Is the Question

15.1 Spread of the Bologna Process

At this point in the discussion, it is important to make clear that no institution of higher learning can be forced to adopt the reforms outlined by the Bologna Process. Institutions can be encouraged strongly to do so, in some instances through the threat of losing government funding; but they cannot be forced. The process must prove itself and also its value, and by 2010 it seems to have succeeded in this effort. Some 47 nations had decided to join, with participation spreading to China, India, African countries, and Latin American countries. A large part of this growing success was attributable to the fact that France, Germany, Italy, and Britain had begun outdrawing the United States in the foreign student market. One obvious reason for doing so was that undergraduate degrees recognized through-out the world could now be earned from European universities after only three years of study for those properly prepared, while U.S. universities continued to require four years of study.

Although concern about this deterioration in the U.S.'s ability to attract foreign students grows, few serious attempts have been made to update our education system. One might suppose that this lack is due to our previously mentioned love affair with individualism, both our greatest strength and our greatest weakness, each university doing things its own way, a "me–I" mentality dominating rather than the "me–we" mentality that is driving Europe's Bologna Process. Quite simply, the Bologna Process with its emphasis on integration and standardization does not yet fit the U.S. mindset.

At least partially as a result of this attitude, when we look at key areas of concern, it becomes obvious that European nations are dealing with shortcoming more rapidly and comprehensively than the United States. In terms of mobility, or the ability of students to study at universities in other European countries and to transfer credits successfully, the Bologna Process has spawned international cooperation while the United States still leaves it up to the individual institution to decide what will be accepted and what won't. In terms of life-long learning, European nations have recognized it as a critical part of their education offering, a key contributor to economic and social development, and, through the Bologna Process, are working to develop a model. In the United States, while many schools have versions of their own, versions that vary widely, emphasis on life-long learning still lies relatively low on the priority list.

In terms of quality assurance, or the ongoing evaluation of course content in terms of workplace and societal needs, efforts are ongoing in European nations with those involved moving toward a universal approach. The United States, on the other hand, has just recently mounted a serious effort to identify what quality in terms of program and course content should entail and how to measure it. In terms of doctoral candidate training, European universities are again trying to define universal standards while integrating efforts between universities and between the departments of individual universities. In the United States, doctoral-level programs have traditionally been one of the strengths of the education system, although institutions have not yet begun encouraging the integration of learning being encouraged in Europe. Also, a growing percentage of PhD candidates who come to U.S. universities from other countries now plan to return to those countries once their training is complete, thus depriving the United States of the expertise these students have gained.

In terms of social needs, while European nations are mounting a serious effort through the Bologna Process to ensure that students qualified to enter universities and graduate programs are not denied the opportunity owing to financial constraints, the United States is currently headed in the opposite direction with the cost of education at all levels rising steadily so that more and more potential students are being denied the opportunity while most of those willing to pay are graduating deep in debt.

15.2 Downsides of the Bologna Process

The European drive to standardize program curriculum, course content, progress requirements, and evaluation systems spearheaded by the Bologna Process has obviously generated many benefits and helped participating countries to compete more successfully. Despite these benefits, however, such standardization has a downside, actually, a number of downsides. Primarily, it can further limit the recognition and development of individual student potential. It also limits the flexibility enjoyed by teachers. In order to achieve the desired results, teachers are forced to "teach to the test," falling victims, once again, to Fredrick Taylor's Scientific Management approach.

In terms of designing universal curriculum, a major problem is that the world being studied is constantly changing. The evolution of history is constant; important changes are occurring almost daily even in the basics of physics, chemistry, biology; in mathematics; in literature; in world geography. In order for a universal curriculum to remain beneficial, it needs to be continually updated.

In terms of universal course testing, to design tests for every subject and to keep those tests updated would be an extremely labor-intensive task. In England, where this approach was implemented in the primary education sector during the late 1990s, owing to the enormity of the challenge, the involved testing was eventually boiled down to three subjects—English, mathematics, and science. Test scores improved for several years, then leveled off (Wyse and Torrance, p. 222). Does this mean that students could do no better? Or, does it mean that if teachers had been given more flexibility in both teaching and testing student performance on the course tests could have continued to improve?

Finally, there is once again the issue of student cooperation. The Bologna Process course testing and final examination systems are designed to discover where students stand as individuals so that the future opportunities they should be afforded can be determined. But the arrangement does not encourage cooperation between students, and such cooperation is beneficial in that those involved learn more by supporting each other's learning, their energy being pooled to create new energy, a process called "synergy." Also, in a cooperative environment students learn to work together and to complement each other, skills important in the workplace where cooperation is increasingly being encouraged, where group rather than individual performance is more frequently being rewarded.

So, the question must be, can the course testing and final examination system developed by the Bologna Process be modified, or can a new evaluation system be designed that also encourages cooperation among students?

Although Europe has taken the lead in terms of educational reform through the initial efforts of the EU, then through those of the European Commission, and then through the Bologna Process, it has not been easy. Progress in effort to unify Europe's key continental sectors was initially made in the economic and political realms. Concerning moderniza- tion of the education system however, it has been a bit slower. The EU's initial desire concerning education was to delineate a universal view of education's role in society, how education systems should be organized and run, and how to define and ensure education quality. Quickly, however, the initial idealism spawned by the EU architects dissolved in the face of eco nomic considerations. Emphasis in the movement shifted from sharing common societal values toward making European universities attractive to tuition-paying students from other parts of the world as a means of gaining income. In order to do so successfully one of the key requirements, as has been said, was to standardize course content so that students not only from other European nations but from foreign coun- tries as well Asian, the United States, Russia, African, South American—could gain credit that would be recognized at home.

A major problem with this strategy, however, arose imme- diately. The uniqueness of what a school offered and how the school made its offering were key determinants of its repu- tation. The standardization of diploma requirements would destroy, or at least lessen, this uniqueness. It would also help eliminate the competition that drove universities to improve and to create offerings that others lacked.

The schools with better reputations, as would be expected, opposed this idea. As an alternative to the development of across-the-continent standards some universities came together, establishing their own limited consortia where they discussed areas of study and curricula. Eight universities— including Oxford, the Sorbonne, and Bologna—created one such consortia called *Europeaum* (Tomusk, p. 89).

Another major problem that the initial idealism of the Bologna Process encountered was political. Eastern European nations seeking entrance into the EU saw adop- tion of the Bologna Process educational philosophy as a ticket for acceptance, doing whatever was necessary to meet the requirements, sometimes fudging results. Adopting the Bologna Process model also helped improve the image of their education sector; "Bologna Process" being a concept in good currency. Emphasis in these countries was too often on "playing the game" necessary to gain admittance rather than on adopting and teaching the values espoused.

15.3 Research in European Universities

Moreover, there is the matter of research. How should it be fit into the Bologna Process model? Prior to the 1700s, most intellectual exchange that occurred was generated by individuals working on their own rather than through institutions of higher learning. The tremendous advances in almost every area—pure science, philosophy, agriculture, industrial technology, navigation, warfare—that occurred during the following decades, however, forced the academic community to reassess its role. Educational institutions obviously needed to continue training students to meet current economic and social needs. The question was how could these institutions, through research, at the same time contribute meaningfully to the development of new possibilities? Where should the emphasis lie, especially at the university and graduate levels? Should it lie on teaching, on research, or on what combination of the two?

Two basic approaches were proposed. The first was that universities should combine research and learning. An outspoken advocate of this approach was the German, Alexander Von Humboldt, who reformed the University of Berlin in the early 1800s, insisting that students should learn by working on research projects and professors should not spend their time delivering information but should teach by facilitating students' research efforts. The problem with this model was that as the size of university classes grew (sound familiar?), providing individual attention became increasingly difficult. As a result of this phenomenon, emphasis began swinging away from research and back toward classroom teaching through lectures.

The second approach was to separate the two pursuits. Teaching would be continued at universities while research would be pursued at *academies.* Again, cultural variations were found. The French, for example, initially did little to encourage research but continued to provide learning in their universities. Only as a result of World War II did the French government create a system of separate research institutes. In these institutions, employees had no teaching responsibilities. They focused solely on research projects. Animosity arose quickly between the two sectors. University professors resented the fact that while they continued to grind out class after class, those working at research institutes could work on whatever they wanted, having no real responsibilities. Researchers, for their part, derided the lack of intellectual stimulation found in the university environment.

Eventually, the line between teaching and research began to blur so that research units began forming relationships with universities. "Teaching" professors began working with the research units while research staff began taking on teaching responsibilities, leading graduate courses and supervising PhD candidates.

In the modern world, teaching and research have become closely tied. In order to gain promotions and, in many cases, to keep their jobs, university professors now need to complete research and to get the results published. The United States has taken the lead in facilitating such efforts by providing sabbaticals and funding.

15.4 Tuition Free Education and Its Problems

Meanwhile, Europe is now struggling with other problems not unfamiliar to the United States. Because European countries believe education to be a critical input to societal development, they attempt to make it available to every citizen of every age, tuition-free. As a result, the system is often overwhelmed, the country not providing enough teachers to meet the demand, many of those who are available being inadequately trained. Owing to the involved constraints, little, if any, individual attention can be provided. At the same time, the teachers are responsible for generating time-consuming research.

The EU is seen by many as a possible instrument for positive change. Its purpose is to make Europe as a whole stronger by encouraging integration of economic systems, border policies, and planning efforts. Education is considered important to this effort. The European Commission, created by the EU to improve education, has provided EU monies to fund multinational research projects tackling education issues. The European Research Council and the European Institute for Innovation and Technology have also been formed, helping the involved scholars gain an overview of the European education system and its issues.

On the student level, the previously mentioned Erasmus Program was created in 1987, funding master's degree programs developed jointly by two or more countries. The program has since paid for thousands of European students to study three months to one academic year in a European country other than their own. One of the major benefits of this program is seen as a broadening of the students' cultural perspective. Jean Monnet Endowed Chairs have also been established to subsidize the work of professors studying European integration.

The role of public sector education, therefore, in terms of the EU's ultimate objective of unification, is currently threefold. In terms of culture, it is to take the lead in creating a common identity, a common set of values that students accept and build their futures on. In terms of politics, it is to foster integration in the continent-wide decision-making process, to give students the knowledge and skills necessary to achieve this. Its third role is to help strengthen Europe's presence as a player on the world stage and to help spread the EU's values and culture eastward.

15.5 How Private School Education in European Countries Is Financed

Up to this point in our discussion of the European education system, emphasis has been on the public sector. Private institutions, however, also play a role. The percentage of students attending private schools in countries considered part of the developed world varies from as much as almost 100% in countries such as Ireland where religion plays a dominant role, to almost 0% in mainly Protestant countries, such as the Scandinavian countries, where religion plays a much less important role (UNESCOM, 2005). Funding sources for private schools also vary greatly. Some of the most exclusive are funded solely through tuition and other private or church contributions. Applicants are screened. Only those with specific characteristics are allowed to attend and school-generated scholarships are being offered to students whose families cannot afford the tuition fee.

While federal funding is not normally available to private schools in the United States, it is frequently available in European countries. In some of these countries, private schools receive the same level of funding as public schools. No tuition or other fees are required. These are called "grant-aid schools." But, at the same time, applicants are not screened. Any student in these countries who desires to attend a grant-aid private school can do so. In other instances, students pay a low fee and the government covers the rest.

Concerning who makes organization and curriculum decisions in the private system where the government covers a majority of costs (the grant-aid system), government representatives or a government-appointed board makes most of them. Generally, however, as the amount of tuition paid by families for education goes up, so does the level of community, parent, and/or church involvement. Also, at this point in history, the belief is growing in many European nations that decisions made concerning both public and private schools should in no case be totally controlled by a government-appointed body, no matter what the level of financial support received, that increased input from communities and parents would be beneficial.

15.6 The Move toward Decentralization

As a result, the current movement in Europe seems to be toward decentralization of power from the government-controlled education bureaucracy toward communities and their schools. The slowness of the bureaucracy in delivering decisions; its inability to encourage or even accept needed change; and its unwillingness to accept input from those doing the teaching and those being taught, all these factors have created a growing amount of frustration and growing calls for the decentralization of decision-making power in both the public and private sectors. Mimicking the charter school concept in the United States, advocates of such changes are calling for greater amounts of school autonomy, for individual schools to take the lead in improving their operation and offerings, though government should still provide funding.

Thus, at the same time that the European Committee and Bologna Process are encouraging increased standardization, the schools in many European nations are seeking increased autonomy. The question is, "Are both objectives possible to achieve at the same time? Can the two be integrated in a beneficial manner?" The most obvious answer is to encourage representatives of the schools themselves to play a larger role in standardizing both curriculum and student progress measurement tools. In a growing number of countries, including France and Spain, "school councils" that include parents and other local stakeholders have been introduced to provide input and to help make decisions concerning school finances, the recruitment of school teachers and staff, student and teacher evaluation, and curricula improvement.

Chapter 16

Standardization as a Threat: The Japanese Experience

16.1 Japan's Individuality Crisis

While both the United States and Europe are striving for greater standardization of education policy, between states in the first instance and between members of the EU in the second, both need to proceed with caution. Standardization can be overdone, as it was during the early Industrial Revolution. During that period, standardization of curriculum spilled over to standardization of student learning habits, standardization of student behavior, standardization of students' lives owing to the efforts of factory owners to turn schools into generators of "well-oiled machine parts" devoid of individuality, students being trained not so much to think as to do what they were programmed to do.

In the world's academic community, perhaps the best example of standardization being carried to a detrimental extreme is Japan. Education systems tend to mirror the characteristics of the culture they serve. In the United States, our system seems to be constantly at war with itself, those seeking standardization battling those who encourage creative and individualized thought; those wanting to ensure that every student reaches a level at which he or she can contribute economically battling the idealists who believe that the development of individual potential is more important; an uneasy balance between differing schools of thought being reached that sways back and forth.

Japan's defining characteristics have to do with self-identity and the sense of individuality that underlie the human decision-making process. A strong sense of individuality is necessary for the development and maintenance of identity and personal autonomy. It is what allows us to break with tradition, causes us to take responsibility for our actions and makes us do the right thing rather than the easy thing. Individuality is necessary for the proper functioning of a democratic state. It is what allows people to speak out when they believe that something wrong is happening.

In addition to this, individuality is what gives people the confidence to strike out on their own, to be entrepreneurs, to think creatively, and to pursue as of yet undiscovered solutions. It is a fundamental element in the formula for change. Without individuality, there can be no creativity, no innovation. When positive change is being sought, another necessary characteristic is dynamism. Without the development of individual potential, such dynamism is impossible to achieve. For these reasons, individuality is a necessary resource for people, cultures, and countries existing in the modern world.

It goes without saying that individuality exists in Japan. Every person possesses it to some degree. The difference is that, in Japan, expressions of individuality, especially in public, are subordinate to expressions of group consensus. This is the result both of Japan's isolated nature and of a process that began centuries ago during Japan's feudal era. Bordered on every side by the ocean and inhabited by a seemingly homogeneous race of people all of whom, according to legend, descended from the sun-goddess, Amaterasu, it is not difficult to see how the distinction between natives and "gaijin" (literally outside person) is of primary importance.

During Japan's agricultural/feudal era, everyone belonged to an "ie." Literally translated, "ie" means house, but this concept was unique in that members outside the family could be adopted into an ie. There were also many levels of "ie" to which one belonged. There was the ie composed mostly of family members; there was the village ie. But, regardless of which *ie* membership one spoke of, it was the membership itself that provided identification to outsiders and thereby functioned as the foundation of all identity.

16.2 A History of "Honne" Bowing to "Tatemae"

Social relations in Japan have also been defined historically by strictly regimented hierarchies. Much of this stems from the adoption of Chinese Confucianism as the dominant religion along with the early militarism of the empire. The Warring States Period sufficed to firmly entrench the importance of hierarchies as each "daimyo," or territorial lord, competed with those around him, jockeying for power and position in a countrywide power struggle that factionalized the population. It was not until the Meiji Restoration in the late 1800s that the notion of a unified Japanese nation arose, a nation defined by its unique characteristics, universal goals, and shared destiny.

At least partially as a result of this history, individuality in Japan is thought of as a "hidden flower" that should be concealed and rarely shown. It is not to be expressed publicly. The resulting suppression takes place in the interest of maintaining harmony and keeping systems and interactions running smoothly. What is done in public must be consistent with accepted and prescribed values, must not create discord, and should promote the good of the nation according to officially recognized guidelines. For this reason, Japanese cultural beliefs split the individual into two parts, the "tatemae" and the "honne." "Tatemae" describes the attitude one must exhibit in dealing with others. It can be translated as outer, explicit, front, or face. "Honne" is the real feelings harbored within the person. It is variously translated as inner, implicit, back, and mind. What is important to this discussion is that the Japanese stress the importance of tatemae to the extent that the public expression of honne can incur undesirable consequences. Functionally, what this means is that socially acceptable attitudes, defined by the groups to which one belongs, are considered a larger, more appropriate, and more important part of one's personality than individual beliefs or feelings. Group identity trumps individual identity.

This trend not only exists in the Japanese education system but is sustained by it. From the year they start nursery school until they graduate from high school, students in Japan are expected to concentrate primarily not on learning how to understand complex issues, or on how to communicate effectively, or even on acquiring the knowledge they will need to succeed in institutions of higher learning. Rather, students are conditioned from day one in how to be Japanese. This training focuses on engendering traits, including the loyalty and perseverance they will need in order to adjust to the obligations faced as adults. The absorption of academic information and the taking of tests on this information are only supporting activities, for the major goal of education in Japan is not to deliver and instill knowledge but to program into students the habit of obedience to the group (Kerr, p. 285).

The result of this approach is a culture that, though it appears harmonious, teaches and sometimes forces individuals to sacrifice their freedoms and individuality to the standards of the group. Students become submissive and subservient, which is exactly what the bureaucrats want. The supposed peacefulness that results from this phenomenon makes people easier to control so that the system does not have to change or adapt. It is in schools that a majority of this conditioning takes place (Kerr qtd. Miyamoto, p. 285).

The bureaucrats who run the nation are products of this same education system. They have also been trained to adhere to group norms rather than to think progressively. Now, however, faced with a world defined by information and communication technologies, one in which the ability to mobilize a productive workforce pales next to the ability to inspire a creative one, Japan is finding its approach to be inadequate.

16.3 The Perils of Importing Progress

In many ways the Japanese culture remains the same as it was during the mid-1800s. The arrival of Commodore Matthew Perry in 1854 showcased how far behind Japan had fallen technologically. This was an unmistakable threat and an affront to the still feudal Japanese government that had, until Perry's visit, exercised near total control over the population. The modernization that followed came at a frenzied pace. Political leaders felt an urgent need to fight their way out of the subordinate political and economic position they had been forced into on the world stage. They needed the tools of the modern world in order to catch up. Among these tools was universal education.

But while the country spent much of its energy between the years of 1853 and 1920, and then again following World War II, on attempts to modernize, something was always missing. As Japan began importing goods, technologies, and education models from other countries, those in power often disregarded the context that originally gave rise to these imports. They did not understand that machines were more than a collection of parts working together to shape a certain product, and that an education system was not just teaching an adopted set of goals and practices. They missed an essential property, the cultural background from which these imports sprang and into which they fit. One might say that the Japanese were importing the image of modernization without the necessary content, and then were trying to force-fit what they had imported into their own value system (Smith, p. 52).

This process was known as "wakon yosai" (Asian values, Western technology). The problem was that it inevitably led to misunderstandings, misapplications, and cultural conflicts. Many of the borrowed technologies, divorced from the cultural soil that had spawned and nurtured them, mutated in unpredictable and sometimes sinister ways. It was like introducing not one, but hundreds, of new species into an ecosystem where any one of them might upset the balance with unpredictable consequences.

> "In the case of education wakon yosai involved a marriage between the old feudal desire for total control (wakon) and compulsory education introduced from the West (yosai). Standardized textbooks, uniforms, school rules, marching in lockstep around the school grounds, bowing in unison—these regimens were able to achieve what 350 years of isolation could not; a triumph over regionalism and individuality. It was probably Japan's single most serious modern adaptation" (Kerr, p. 283).

16.4 The Samuraization of Workers and Students

Japan's leaders, at this point, imported relatively wholesale the Prussian education system, including details such as the military style uniforms. But, true to its wakon yosai approach to consumption of the modern, the societal values that came along as part of the imported system were replaced with those of the Japanese ruling class. The value of education was perceived mainly to be its ability to thrust Japan into the fray of the industrial era. And, initially, it helped do just that. Rather than agricultural workhorses, lower class citizens were now educated to become cogs in the industrial engine of the country. This redefinition of responsibility was in no way traceable to the respect for individuality that had eventually helped shape the development of universal education in Western nations. Instead, the adoption of universal education in Japan was rooted in the ruling class' continuing desire to maximize the economic value of the peasantry, if not in the fields, then in the factories.

This change of roles was achieved through a façade of enfranchisement whereby an entire section of the population, members of which, until this point, had not even been allowed to possess a family name to accompany their given name, was now told that it directly served the emperor and the great nation of Japan. Subservient social classes that had for centuries been excluded from the affairs of state were now called upon to act as the nation's new samurai. They were told that they belonged to a great empire for whose fate they had been made responsible.

This "samuraization" of the common people was nowhere more evident than in the new education system. The country's first education minister, Arinori Mori, voiced this mood when he talked about the system's purpose as being the manufacture of people needed by the state, rather than of individuals well versed in the arts and sciences. He wanted graduates for whom duty came first, who would willingly sacrifice their lives if called upon to do so. Education was seen not as a child's right, but as a duty of parents to make sure their children received the proper programming and adopted the proper attitude (Smith, p. 71).

It is not hard to see how such a process could easily spin out of control and result in children lining up in school yards to shout "Banzai!" When the first graduates of the new education system took their place in society during the early 1930s, they carried with them an attitude that resulted in the formation of the "kenpeitai," or secret police, in censorship, and in fanaticism. Ultra-nationalist sentiments deepened among the masses while the power and influence of the privileged elite continued to expand, turning Japan against her neighbors and inevitably leading to war (Kerr, p. 284).

Although Japan had become a powerful nation, it had also become unstable and dangerous to itself. Its eventual collapse was tremendously damaging. Its attempt to modernize without first developing socially and culturally should serve as a potent warning against the importation and implementation of changes (such as the Bologna Process) that have not adapted to support into cultures them. The only way to be certain that such changes become functional is to allow them to emerge naturally as the culture, society, and zeitgeist of a nation develop according to their own volition.

16.5 A Lost Opportunity

The unfortunate tendency of Japan to consume modernity rather than to truly modernize continued following World War II. It is impossible to say with any degree of certainty whether or not the failure of the nation's first modernization attempt, that triggered by Commodore Perry's visit, was the result of its natural development having been cut short by a forced opening to the West. Responsibility for the undesired outcome of Japan's second modernization revolution, however, falls squarely upon the shoulders of foreigners who tried to change the culture without first understanding it. The attempt to democratize and liberalize Japan following World War II was led by General Douglas MacArthur of the United States. It was referred to by the occupation forces as "revolution from above" and by many Japanese, at least initially, as "gifts from heaven."

Although very few of Japan's wartime leaders remained, and even fewer were willing to question the decisions of the occupying forces, Yoshida Shigeru, who served as Prime minister from 1946 to 1947 and again from 1948 to 1954, belittled efforts to make Japan democratic saying that the Japanese people were incapable of governing themselves. He added that Americans who argued to the contrary were suffering from ethnocentrism (Dower, p. 84).

While such statements might reflect the bitterness of a leader who had lost his power, they may also contain some truth. A successful democracy requires a fertile culture in which to grow and energy provided by its citizens to nurture that growth. Even ardent supporters of the new democracy had their doubts, fearing that the common people were too beaten up from the war to mount the effort necessary to establish a successful democracy. At the same time, the old guard had not been uprooted and obviously had no intent of changing its behavior (Dower, p. 84).

In the end, however, these doubts did not really matter. Japan was never given the opportunity to find out whether or not it could succeed as a democracy. Following a brief stint during which the G.H.Q. (those in charge of the American occupation) actually worked to help Japan embrace democracy and human rights, a marked reversal occurred. As a result of the looming Cold War, it was decided in Washington that Japan must quickly be made ready to serve the role designated by its conquerors. This change of mind is called "the reverse course." The U.S. occupiers had come to Japan with the intent on remaking that country in their own image. Instead, they further entrenched the very hierarchical, identity-subsuming power structure that had derailed the culture in the first place.

The consequences of the reverse course affected everyone, but it was the young who would pay the steepest price. Under the guise of education reform, they had been left in the care of an elitist, nationalistic bureaucracy. In 1946, a US Education Mission had been sent to Japan to complete an analysis and to give advice. The Mission's report stated that the problems of the prewar system had included excessive centralization; multitrack schooling; uniform and knowledge-dissemination-based teaching; a bureaucratic, authoritarian administration, and the complexity of the Japanese writing systems (Okano, p. 30).

Considering what happened during the reverse course, it comes as no surprise that every one of these problems remains today. Here are some of the reasons why, briefly, things have failed to change: (1) School boards and representatives are appointed by the Ministry of Education with no input from local communities; (2) Students are separated into different tracks based entirely upon a test administered at the end of their three years in middle school that determines their future employment and social status (Smith, p. 88); (3) All students of a given age group are taught the same lesson in the same way on the same day throughout Japan (Kerr qdt Reischauer, p. 288); (4) The Ministry of Education reviews all textbooks and standardizes their content. Textbooks may not mention divorce, single-parent families, late marriage, or pizza, the Ministry having decided that pizza is not an acceptable meal for families; (5) The writing system still consists of two different alphabets in addition to 2000 Chinese characters (the minimum required for literacy), all of which are taught through rote memorization (Kerr, pp. 295–296).

16.6 Japan Goes to War in the Marketplace

The reverse course also set the stage for plunging Japan back into war, but on a new battlefield. This time the conflict was played out in the arena of capitalism. One of the first Japanese officials to visit the United States announced that capitalism was remarkably like, "warfare conducted in peace time." Since the new constitution of the country (the one drafted by the GHQ) forbid Japan from engaging in military endeavors outside the country's borders, the leaders responsible for Japan's role in World War II, upon being reinstated, changed their sights and geared up to wage a new type of war, this one on the economic battlefield.

The ammunition used was once again the country's young men and women. The nation's subsequent approach to education was based on the previously mentioned human–capital theory, a concept made popular by the U.S. Robber Barons. The belief that the value of education lies in the economic returns it provides was interpreted in Japan to mean that students should be trained to follow instructions without allowing creative thought to interfere, another concept popular with the Robber Barons and their champions. As a result, education in Japan became a tool used to produce a willing and pliable workforce of "corporate warriors" who were adept, above all, at taking orders. The belief was that an aggressive economy based on mass-production requires a few strong leaders at the top and a vast army of foot soldiers who will serve loyally in the war for economic dominance (Smith, p. 97). It is certainly no exaggeration to compare the Japanese workplace to a battlefield, its participants to soldiers. As proof of this assertion, one might point to the estimated 10,000 employees who currently die each year from the stress of overwork (Smith, p. 115).

Such cultural overemphasis on standardization and control begins with the education system. As has already been mentioned, there is an international epidemic of stimulus–response style education and, despite efforts at control and modernization, it continues to spread. Students in many countries are still trained to memorize instead of to question. As a result, they learn obedience to authority and that the establishment possesses, not only all of the correct answers, but the right to punish those whose do not respond with those answers. In Japan, this tradition is more prevalent than in most other countries. The Confucian ethic that provides direction for social interaction prescribes strict relationships between parents and children, managers and employees, as well as teachers and students. People know where they stand in relation to one another, such positioning shaping their contribution to any social interaction. One's behavior is a function of one's position. The result is a kind of formalized inequality that defines one's limits of personal expression. Teachers, for example, speak, students listen.

16.7 Does Excessive Regimentation Support a Hidden Curriculum in the Classroom?

While this high degree of organization does, of course, produce positive results—for example, allowing Japan to enjoy one of the lowest crime rates in the industrialized world and the solidarity with which the population faces unexpected disasters—in terms of education it ends up doing more harm than good. One of the most important aspects of learning that we must understand if we are to truly comprehend the individual education process is that our brains never stop processing data and information. Everything we do, every stimulus that we are exposed to causes changes and generates learning of some sort. As a result of this realization, we must account for the effects of a hidden curriculum and the hidden lessons being taught in our classrooms and by our education systems.

If a student does well on a test and, as a result, receives a high grade, that grade, the approval expressed by teachers and parents, the reaction of classmates are all part of the education process, along with the initial input digested while preparing for the test. The student learns that his or her effort has produced a good grade along with the accompanying positive or negative reinforcement. Therefore, we are not simply supplying students with the information that they need in order to pass the test; we are teaching them an entire value system. Students who do well are being conditioned to believe that the grade received for their effort is the desired reward rather than the learning itself, and that remembering the information received is a path to rewards rather than its own reward.

Unfortunately, once this conditioning is in place, if no grade will be received for learning something, the motivation to learn fades. This is one of the reasons why, in Japan's heavily test-centric culture, education generally ends with college graduation. Students want the grades and degrees necessary to gain employment and little else. Continuing adult education is extraordinarily rare, as are graduate school enrollments with Japan recording fewer than almost any other industrialized nation. A second reason for this circumstance is that companies rarely encourage employees at any level to continue their education. Immediate productivity is the objective, and the time and energy spent doing schoolwork might detract from that productivity.

16.8 Competition Out of Control

However, there is an even more sinister aspect to Japan's education system. Though success is rewarded, on a more fundamental level it is a system built on punishment. Even students who do well are routinely subjected to red pen comments and grade deductions for incorrect answers, both of which are intrinsically punishing forms of feedback. Learning is a process characterized, not by striving to succeed, but by the attempt to avoid being punished. Even the greatest success, avoiding all punishment, leads only to more potential punishment. Rather than inspiring them to try harder, this system kills the motivation of even the most successful students as they progress from being outgoing and exuberant in elementary school to shutting down and being unwilling to ask questions or to actively engage in discussions by the time they reach high school. Years of being punished for every mistake make them afraid to try.

For students who are less successful, the prognosis is even worse. If they persevere for long enough, they might be able to graduate from high school and possibly even college. But in such a competitive and hierarchical society, their opportunities will be limited. Those who simply do not fit into the standardized definition of "intelligent" often finish school junior high school but then are unwilling to attempt or unable to pass the tests necessary to continue their education. In this way, the system effectively creates a whole class of 14-year-old educational have-nots destined to exist on the socio-economic fringes.

Parents who want to prevent this from happening to their child look for every educational advantage. Gaining entrance to the right school can make all the difference but, as a result, such institutions are in high demand. The school's solution is an entrance exam to determine which students will be admitted. Dependency on such testing has saturated the society, tests being administered to younger and younger students. It is now possible to find nursery schools that require their toddler-aged applicants to pass a competitive entrance exam measuring their academic aptitude.

The entrance exam system has become so entrenched and currently wields so much power that, at times, it appears as though the entire educational process now exists to support it. Often starting during elementary school, students seeking an advantage attend extra classes at *cram schools* designed to prepare them for these exams. Compared to other developed nations, Japan spends very little per capita on education. But once the cost of cram courses is factored in, Japan tops the list for per-capita expense, an average family spending more than half of its income on child education, both formal and informal.

Eighty percent of students have failed at least one entrance exam by the age of 15, a potent reminder for most of the country's teens that they just aren't good enough. Once Japanese students reach college, with no entrance exams to prepare for, however, many treat it as a vacation. Their graduation is virtually guaranteed, as evidenced by a recent rash of parents suing universities that displayed the audacity to fail their children. The grades issued at this level are too often based, not on participation or on the quality of work pro- duced, but on attendance. Even the students who do show up frequently treat classes as an opportunity to catch up on their sleep, or as an opportunity to enrich their social lives.

Chapter 17

Japan's Inability to Modernize Its Education System

17.1 The Toll Taken by Excessive Standardization

Returning to the idea of a hidden curriculum, Japan's highly standardized hierarchical approach has the effect of encouraging a very specific way of thinking, of encouraging a very specific value system. Just as a science question has an answer and the teacher knows it, questions such as "How should I act in public?" "How should I dress?" and "What should I value?" are also assumed to have singular, easily defined answers possessed by one's social superiors. This is evident throughout the Japanese education system. Students must wear matching uniforms. They must change from their thin summer to their thicker winter uniforms on a specific day prescribed by the school well in advance and, therefore, on a day not at all dependent upon weather conditions. Students are often prevented from working part-time jobs or using a non-approved route to walk to school.

When conducting exams for admission to a higher-level institution, teachers are known to walk around, inspecting students for evidence of pierced ears, hair that has been dyed any color other than black, nail polish, or bad attitudes. Students who display any of these aberrations are not allowed to move up, no matter what their score. Some schools have also been known to distribute postexam surveys to students under the guise of gauging honest and confidential reactions to admission procedures. Upon collection, however, responses are matched to respondents and carefully reviewed. Any student who has expressed displeasure is dropped from the applicant pool.

This is all evidence of a type of standardization that extends well beyond testing. It has become a defining feature of the system as a whole for, as we know, culture defines and is defined by education in equal measures. A culture that attempts to standardize its people will institute a standardized education system that produces students who support, perpetuate, and more deeply entrench the existing cultural mores.

17.2 Those Who Suffer the Most

Let us, now turn our attention to the students who lack the necessary attitude to succeed and have fallen through the cracks. Sometimes a student is simply too different, too much of an individual to succeed in the traditionally defined academic sense. Often these students are subjected to severe bullying at the hands of other students. Such bullying, however, differs markedly from that exhibited in Western countries. Japan's "ijime" is characterized by a form of institutionalized bullying that is often overlooked or even endorsed by school faculty because it serves the purpose of reinforcing the normative, behavioral-standardization agenda. Being too tall, too short, too smart, too effeminate, too skilled at sports … any noticeable difference can be enough to justify bullying, such behavior being considered acceptable because the one being bullied is defined as the one at fault. One of Japan's best-known sayings, "The nail that sticks out gets hammered," embodies the sentiments of most schools and often that of the culture as a whole (Kerr, pp. 291–292).

As for the victims, they either conform or are forced out. The Japanese word "hikkikomori" means "to pull away and shut off." This word and definition are used to represent what happens to some individuals when the organized conditioning, instructive bullying, and social pressure all fail to produce the desired result. The hikkikomori are the silent, identity-less individuals who fall out of the system and off the grid because fitting in is something they cannot or will not do. There are now an estimated 3,600,000 such hikkikomori throughout Japan, locked away in their rooms for years at a time. They spend their days surfing the Internet, reading comic books, playing games, and rarely interacting with even those closest to them. Often provided for by concerned parents, the hikkikomori are unable and unwilling to face the society that looms so threateningly outside their walls (Zielenziger, 2006).

Not many resources are available to people who fall out of the system in this way. Mental health professionals are scarce in Japan. Few of the needy would feel comfortable seeking such help anyway because doing so would invite further stigmatization. Often, those closest to a hikkikomori refuse to assist or to even publicly acknowledge that the problem exists for fear that they will be associated with the sufferer and stigmatized as well. So the hikkikomori languish in despair and silence, knowing that their only crime is being different and not fitting the mold.

Other so-called misfits turn their frustrations with the enforced standardization of youth outwards. Rather than withdrawing from society like the hikkikomori, they attack it. Among teenagers, membership in "bosozoku," or motor-cycle gangs, is growing, along with the incidence of crimes associated with these groups. Bosozoku exist to fight, often employing weapons such as baseball bats and knives, and orchestrating attacks on each other. It is not unusual for such attacks to end fatally. They are also known for random attacks against pedestrians and motorists, for committing robberies, and for other such apparently random acts of violence.

Yet the label, "random" in this situation, is a misnomer. These are teenagers who have been beaten down and crushed from a very young age by a system of extreme expectation and competition. Every success has meant only that more was expected of them; every failure let the entire family down. Before they were able to develop an idea of who they were or what they wanted to do, these young people were told who they needed to be and what they needed to achieve. Bosozoku are angry and alienated. Having been treated like industrial cogs since an early age, they are seeking an outlet for self-expression. Over 1000 motorcycle gangs now exist throughout Japan. The judicial system still levies only minor punishments for juvenile offenders, like a holdover from the days when most juvenile crimes were petty theft. Even a crime such as murder often warrants only a few months in reform school. The gangs serve as recruiting pools for Japan's organized crime syndicates, the "Yakuza."

Of course, gangs of young people are common around the world. One of the major differences, however, is that in Japan, most of these youths come, not from the lower socio-economic classes, but from middle class, stable families, and good neighborhoods. They have never wanted for anything material, but are the products of a system that leaves them existentially deprived, that strips them of their individuality, and leaves them desperate for a way to define their existence and to feel powerful in the face of uncertainty.

17.3 More Disturbing Evidence

This same motivation is behind an even more disturbing trend, that of Japan's teenage killers. In the last 20 years, a grisly number of murders have been committed by children between the ages of 8 and 17. Often these affairs have involved students killing their classmates, their teachers, or their parents. In one of the most famous cases, known as the *Kobo Killer* case, a 14-year-old boy murdered a 10-year-old female student with a hammer just days before kidnapping an 11-year-old male schoolmate. The younger boy's head was found on the school gate two days later with a note in his mouth. Among other things the note read, "I want to take revenge on the compulsory education system that has made me transparent and invisible."

In a different case, a schoolboy used a 12-inch knife to hold 10 people hostage on a bus for hours before going on a killing frenzy. Once apprehended, it was discovered that he had recently failed a high school entrance exam and was quoted as saying, "If I cannot succeed in an orthodox way, at least I can succeed as a criminal." In the same month, a 16-year-old put a sleeping commuter into a coma by striking him repeatedly with a hammer and a 17-year-old broke into an elderly woman's house and bludgeoned her to death. In June 2004, an 11-year-old girl armed with a box cutter brutally murdered a 12-year-old classmate who had reportedly called her "prissy" and "overweight" on a website. The killer, it turned out, was extremely upset because her parents had forced her to quit the basketball team in order to focus more on studies. There are cases in which school children have killed their teachers after being scolded about their grades. There are cases where they have also killed their parents for the same offense.

Children are not the only ones cracking under the pressure of ultra-competitiveness. A housewife, upset that her neighbor's two-year-old daughter had been admitted to a prestigious elementary school and her own child had not, strangled the young girl. When the story went public, newspapers received a flood of sympathetic letters commiserating, not with the victim's family, but with the murderer. They expressed understanding of the social pressures that had driven her to commit the crime (Hays, 2009). This is not an isolated incident. Police departments and newspaper reports receive similar letters from students around the country concerning the crimes previously detailed. The authors of such letters talk about how they can understand what these killers were going through, how they can envision not being able to deal with the pressure anymore and, eventually, cracking.

A study of 1800 Japanese students found that 20% were afraid that they would go insane and 30% regarded their lives as failures (BBC, 2000). In a disturbing reversal, it is frequently the successful students who are most likely to snap. Rather than dropping out or getting their kicks in a gang, they submit to the continual indoctrination. They are taught that their classmates are enemies bent on taking success away from them. The involved students rarely develop the verbal ability necessary to vent their concerns and frustrations since their education has taught them that critical discussion and questioning are unnecessary and to be avoided. To this situation adds the fact that such students are usually sleep deprived; that the pressure is both constant and building; and we have a formula for sociopathology.

If children are denied their quest for an identity by standardization and are made invisible, they will search for ways to show that they matter. For some, this means continuing to struggle until they succeed in the orthodox manner, no matter what the emotional cost. For others, it will mean acting out in socially unacceptable ways. While for the rest, it will mean just accepting their invisibility until they can bear it no longer.

17.4 The Nation as a Whole Suffers

Let's look at a final example. The consequences of excessively standardized education extend well beyond childhood and adolescence. On March 11, 2011 Japan was hit by what has come to be known as "the triple disaster." An earthquake triggered, a tsunami, and a crisis at the Fukushima No. 1 nuclear power plant. The full extent of the resulting radioactive crisis has yet to be determined, but it is, without a doubt, one of the worst in human history. In July 2012, an independent Diet commissioned to investigate what happened at the plant issued its findings. The report said that, "What must be admitted—very painfully—is that this was a disaster 'Made in Japan.' Its fundamental causes are to be found in the ingrained conventions of Japanese culture: our reflexive obedience; our reluctance to question authority; our devotion to 'sticking with the program'; our groupism; and our insularity (Nagata, 2012)."

According to the report, the plant had repeatedly been found not to meet safety requirements. But collusion between those involved kept the required improvements from being made. The government regulators, when doing their analysis, were acting hand-in-hand with those they were meant to regulate. When the regulators said that nothing needed to be fixed, the decision was passed down the hierarchy and, predictably, everyone below simply accepted it. No one ever spoke up. Following the disaster, it has been alleged that cleanup crews working in the radioactive area around the plant were instructed to cover their radiation meters with lead plates so that they might spend more time in the contaminated area before registering the legal limit for absorbed radiation.

These are two examples of how emphasizing obedience over individuality; how treating students like inanimate cups to be filled with information rather than alive, critical thinkers capable of forming opinions of their own; how to develop in students a fear of standing out, are ill-advised and potentially damaging approaches to education. The irradiated and uninhabitable area of Japan may be located around Fukushima, but the roots of this disaster are in the classroom. The attempt to standardize people has tragic consequences both when it succeeds and when it fails, and is, by any measure, misguided. Today's world does not need standardized people. It needs individuals.

17.5 The Major Obstruction to Change

Despite continuous half-hearted but well-meaning attempts at meeting this challenge through redesign of Japan's approach to education, the traditional system remains in place. The question is, "why?" and the answer has to include "dependency theory." While dependency theory is typically employed to explain the ways in which wealthy countries (the core) control less-developed countries (the periphery) through economic or military power, in Japan there is another means of gaining control—through identity. Central to any understanding of Japanese culture and language are the ideas of "omote" and "ura." These two concepts are closely related to the concepts of tatemae and hone, mentioned earlier, and can be roughly translated to mean outside (omote) and inside (ura). These concepts run throughout the entirety of Japanese language and relationships.

The people of this culture are trained and encouraged to categorize everyone they know or meet into one of these two categories. This process begins at the earliest stages of education when children are assigned to a "kumi" or "group" with which they will remain until graduation, thus facilitating the beginnings of the "us versus them mentality," "them" including anybody outside the group (Kerr qtd. Duke, p. 287). Such standardization is constantly reinforced. Songs, greetings, and announcements are practiced and recited in unison by group members with precise timing. Sports days are marked by the ever-popular 35-person jump rope and the 42-legged race.

These activities are supposedly designed to prepare students for the world they will enter upon graduation. In fact, however, the young people are being prepared instead for the world entered had they graduated in 1955.

The result of such an education and the cultural mores it reflects and sustains is a society composed of groups and cliques in which "who you are" is not nearly as important as "where you belong." The groups into which a Japanese person has been accepted are the labels by which that person is identified. Therefore, group membership is the fundamental ingredient of identity formation, individuals being sheltered by the group (Doi, p. 56).

In dependency theory, from an economic perspective, the core and the periphery are typically the economically privileged and underprivileged in a given relationship. A more developed country will leverage its power and resources to put a less-developed one in a compromising position. This inequitable balance of power serves to reinforce the position of both. In addition, education is often used as a mechanism of control by the core to instill values conducive to the maintenance of the power imbalance.

In Japan, the resource that tips the balance is not economic, but psychological. The suppression of public individuality marginalizes those who do not belong to a group. It is through group membership and participation that individuals find an avenue of public expression. When groups are the only source of identity, therefore, not belonging to a group is tantamount to not having an identity, to not being able to express one's individuality, to not existing.

Just as with other dependency relationships, the Japanese core is concerned with maintaining its power position. Occasionally, doing so requires more than just a monopolistic mentality. This is why anyone who steps outside the group for any reason must suffer the wrath of the other group members, the previously mentioned bullying or ijime. This practice occurs not only in schools, but throughout the culture in every sector and at every level. It involves not only the subjugation of the weak or of individuals on the periphery by the strong, but is also used as a tool by the core group to weed out differences and to inspire sameness among members.

As a result of the dependency relationship, both core group members and individuals on the periphery suffer developmentally. Both are unable to develop their individuality, their potential fully. Core members keep those on the periphery from doing so. But they also keep each other from doing so. Members of the core often purposefully underperform in order not to stand out and attract attention. This type of control is insidious and whereas peripheral groups and even discontented core members in other societies can draw on their native culture, on their anger at being marginalized or bullied, or on their own sense of entitlement to resist the influence of the core, in Japan such resistance is only a way to work oneself into more trouble.

17.6 The Inability to Get beyond Dependency Theory and Its Consequences

The major problem, however, with identity dependence and the suppression of individual development it engenders in Japan is that progress concerning this issue seems to be constantly out of reach. For change in an established cultural order to occur, individuals must express discontent and a leader must emerge to gather and organize support. But the Japanese emphasis on sharing responsibility and obeying decisions of the core on all levels leads to a situation in which nobody is in charge. Not only is no one in charge, but no one wants to take charge since the emergence of such a leader would represent a break with the group. Not only would the individual suffer for his or her indiscretion, but others would feel more acutely than ever the pressure to conform (Kerr, p. 232).

Since the reaction being controlled by group pressure is precisely the reaction required for drastic change, it would appear that the core has established self-perpetuating dominance over the periphery. The periphery and even members of the core can resent secretly and vehemently the hold that groups have on society, but their understanding of the retribution that open opposition will lead to stifles dissent.

A more open form of rebellion might be evidenced by the brain drain occurring in Japan. While this phenomenon has much in common with those experienced by less-developed countries, the level of the Japanese brain drain might suggest "brain exodus" as a more accurate label. Obvious examples of this exodus include Japanese baseball players, prominent doctors, artists, and business leaders who have left their country in search of a culture where they are encouraged to do great things and to pursue success. Historically, this situation is probably unique, that one of the world's most advanced societies is driving its brightest and most talented out owing to an inability to recognize and laud their potential and individual contributions (Kerr, p. 340).

Around the mid-1980s and into the 1990s, an outcry arose among teachers, parents, and business leaders that the education system no longer provided students with the skills necessary to succeed. The catch-word at that point was "individuality." In response, the Japanese government made changes intended to allow students more opportunity to develop personally. The desire was to move away from the "education-as-testing" mentality and to embrace a more holistic approach. Reforms included integrated-studies classes (which in practice were remarkably similar to periods of study hall), and cutbacks in the time spent in school (which no doubt inspired parents to purchase even more supplementary cram school education).

While the public remained displeased with these token efforts, it was the results of the 2003 PISA test that eventually showed the changes to be useless. In mathematics proficiency,

Japanese students slipped to sixth place among OECD countries (Cave). Apparently no one saw the contradiction inherent in basing the evaluation of educational reforms designed to get away from testing on the results of a test. Predictably, responses to this slippage included calls for Japan to revert to the post-war style of education, a style based on hard work, memorization, and testing.

17.7 Is Cultural Reform Possible?

Attempts to reform the system were actually doomed from the start. First, their success in many ways depended on teachers who were products of the same repressive system the reforms sought to change. Second, minor tweaks were made when only a major overhaul would suffice. Third, in order to make a major overhaul, the entire interdependent society, from top to bottom, would need to be reinvented. It needed to be torn down, then rebuilt (Kerr, p. 365).

As is its custom, the bureaucracy responded to growing public concern by issuing "tatemae" proposals—surface-level changes that fail to address the underlying problems, and that were designed mainly to placate critics. When these changes failed as well, their failure was interpreted as further proof that the reforms were wrong-minded, that the traditional, accepted way of educating students was the only way.

In this process, it is not difficult to see, again, the desire of the core to keep its members and the periphery in line. So, in the end, the attempts at educational reform in the interest of individuality achieved what just about all similar attempts involving social systems achieve in Japan—a retrenching of existing ideology and a fresh coat of paint.

Identity dependency in the Japanese culture is self-perpetuating. As time passes, it will become increasingly ingrained as the traditional Japanese way. But it is more a symptom than a life-threatening disease. The illness this societal convention stems from is one of a country trying desperately to convince itself that it is modern when, culturally, the necessary changes have not occurred. In terms of education, the system is still predicated on the assumption that its students exist, not as autonomous beings with individual value and individual contributions to make, but as servants of the state to be programmed as the state sees fit. The nation has been characterized as a bullet train ripping through stages of modernization, industrialization, war, and rebuilding without finding time to experience an awakening of the individual, an awakening of individualism as was experienced in Europe during the Enlightenment Period (Zielenziger, p. 126).

Japan resembles one giant dependency relationship in which education serves to reinforce the core/periphery dynamic. Until the culture develops respect for individual worth, this trend will continue.

The bright side of the picture is that the information age, the technology involved has made it increasingly difficult to hide from what is going on in the rest of the world. One of the major trends in this era of globalization is the increasing importance of the individual. It is now easier than ever for one person to start a business; support a cause; connect to those with power and influence; or simply to engage in free, public self-expression. It will be interesting to see how Japanese society responds to the information pouring in from countries where young people have risen up against those thwarting their efforts at self-improvement. The suspicion grows that the energy stifled for so long by the nation's ossified hierarchies is bound to eventually find a suitable outlet. All of the suppressed individuality will eventually come pouring out and, unlike Japan's previous two revolutions, this one will come, not from the emperor or the bureaucrats or the conquerors, but from the people.

Chapter 18

Things That Need Further Improvement in the United States

18.1 Developing Standards for Academic Achievement at the Highest Level

Meanwhile, turning back to modern time in the United States and our attempts to improve student performance, the two states that led the way concerning consequential accountability and proved its value in terms of encouraging student progress were Texas and North Carolina. The approaches used by these two states, however, differed, especially in terms of interventions. Texas set the same standards for every student, raising the bar incrementally. In terms of rewards and punishments, Texas offered financial benefits to schools that stayed the pace. For those that fell behind, the "punishments" differed somewhat from those stipulated by NCLB. They included the development of student achievement improvement plans, public hearings on the matter, appointment of a school monitor, and, eventually, if things did not improve, a state takeover. The main tactic was to shame these schools into improving.

North Carolina used two measures for judging progress. The first was the measure of each school's progress against a common benchmark. The second measure was improvement in student scores over the course of the school year. In terms of rewards and interventions, North Carolina paid bonuses to the teachers and staff of schools that "exceeded their performance targets by at least ten percent." Only one intervention was used for schools lagging behind. The state sent assistance teams composed of an administrator and several experienced teachers for one year to work daily with the school in order to improve its performance (Grissmer and Flanagan, "Exploring Rapid Achievement Gains…").

In terms of a second major weakness of NCLB—the inability to compare the progress of schools in different states against a universal standard—the Department of Education instituted the *National Assessment of Educational Progress Test*. This test was the first to comparatively measure the progress of school systems in different states so that sense could be made out of what was going on nationally. But, then, if all students take the same test at the end of their secondary school studies, can't test results serve as a basis for comparing school performance in individual states as well? The answer is obviously "yes." With this information in hand, then, the National Assessment of Educational Progress Test and other measures like that can be designed to identify weaknesses in policy, teaching methodology, and administrative systems.

In summation, major efforts are currently underway: (1) to develop a universally acceptable standard and a test based on it that will be used to measure the learning of individual students and (2) to find ways to use results from the same testing vehicle to measure individual school performance so that the teaching and administrative systems of all schools can be assessed, so that those schools not doing well can be given assistance.

18.2 Improving the Performance of Teachers as Well

The United States is attempting to develop accurate ways to measure the performance and progress of both the individual student and the school. But what about teachers? How do we measure the effectiveness of the teachers who so strongly impact the performance of students, who are in large part responsible for the performance of schools as measured against some local, state, or national standard? What kind of rewards should be offered to encourage good teacher's performance? What kinds of assistance should be offered to help improve teachers' performance?

Evaluation of teachers, according to the Obama administration's reasoning, should be based in large part on student class test scores, with a focus on student improvement in English and math. Teacher unions have opposed this approach, and for good reason. A teacher's skill is only one among many factors that affect students' performance, maybe not even the most important. Other factors that have been researched and proved relevant include the number of students in a class, the physical classroom itself, the behavior and attitude of students in the class, the school budget, the neighborhood the school is located in, race, dietary habits of the student and the student's family, the parents' attitude toward education, the amount of time parents spend with the student, sleep habits of the student, whether the student has an after-school job, time spent watching television, wealth of the family, whether the student is involved in sports, and so on. Also, there is an understanding that all students cannot do test well and that tests cannot accurately account for factors such as multiple intelligences and primary learning modalities.

With the above factors in mind, the question we need to ask at this point must obviously be, "Is it possible to factor all relevant variables into the calculation of a student's academic progress or lack thereof?" The answer to this question must obviously be, "No, it is not." So, focusing narrowly on a teacher's ability to facilitate that progress disallows the level of comprehension necessary to a true understanding of the challenge, an understanding which, in turn, is necessary for us to learn how to deal with the challenge. What is becoming increasingly clear is that not only we are having difficulty in designing an accurate measure for student and school progress, but we are also having difficulty in designing one for teachers' contribution to that progress, and, therefore, that the decision to base the teacher's reward on class test results is unfair.

A recent editorial by Bill Gates in *The New York Times Op-Ed* section entitled, *Shame Is Not the Solution*, highlighted a wrong approach being taken by several states, an approach based on punishment rather than on encouragement. The New York State Court of Appeals, for example, recently ruled that evaluations of public school teacher performance could be released. Teachers will apparently be ranked by name. The object is apparently, again, to shame those earning lower rankings into improving their performance.

At primary and secondary school levels, the traditional teacher evaluation system has been based on the class grades earned by students; on occasional, short visits by other faculty or by administrators to the classroom in order to observe performance; and on the input of parents, though this latter factor does not usually have much impact unless the teacher has done something really out of line. There are no teacher evaluations handed in by students. At the elementary school level and, perhaps, at the junior high school level, this is understandable. But one would think that teacher evaluations might be of value at the high school level, giving administrators a better feel for the teacher's performance, as they do at the college level, pointing out both strengths and areas where improvement is needed.

18.3 Teachers as Students

How is such improvement facilitated? Setting universal standards for all students and schools and teachers to strive toward is a good idea and necessary, but it is the relatively easy part. Defining an effective way to facilitate the efforts of students and schools and especially of teachers to meet those standards is the real challenge. Education should be an ongoing process for instructors as well as for students. At this point, however, one must ask how best teachers can be trained to help students realize their potential? There is, of course, continuing education, the requirement for teachers to attend seminars and classes themselves. But is an off-sight college classroom or hotel meeting room the best setting for such educational efforts? Or is the best setting for teacher education "on-the-job"?

"Creativity" occurs, as has been said, when somebody puts the pieces together in a new way that makes a contribution to a field of knowledge. Encouraging creative thought in students has been a goal of academicians since, at least, the publication of Jean Jacques Rousseau's *Emile, or On Education* (1762). But this raises a critical question. If society deems the discovery and encouragement of creative potential in students to be one of the major objectives of our education system, an objective important to its success, why doesn't society stress the same thing for those made responsible for such discovery and such encouragement, for the teachers?

The main responsibility of teachers is instruction of students. Instruction is usually organized by subject or by discipline. When talking about instruction, traditional problems faced by teachers include their own poor preparation; difficulty in generating interest in the subject among students; the inability or unwillingness of teachers to stay up with advances in their field; the inability or unwillingness of teachers to appropriately utilize available technology; the inability of teachers, owing to class size, to pay enough attention to individual students.

One of the ways developed for dealing with these problems and for turning the classroom presentation into a learning experience for the teacher as well as students is through "team teaching." Teachers in the same discipline can work together to enrich their individual lesson plans; teachers in the same discipline can join forces to deliver classes. Sometimes teachers from different disciplines can integrate their efforts and their lesson plans to provide students with a more comprehensive perspective. One of the strengths of this approach is that it allows the involved teachers to feed off each other, to combine their strengths.

Another way to deal with some of the problems cited is to form "professional learning committees." These committees can be put together at any level. They can include teachers from a single discipline. In larger schools, they can include teachers from one grade level for one discipline. They can include teachers from related disciplines. In usually smaller schools, they can be open to teachers from all disciplines. Their purpose is to allow teachers to share their approach to teaching in general; to allow them to share how they deal with specific situations; to allow them to share resources, knowledge, new ideas, and problems; and to encourage them to support each other. Such committees can meet formally with a predefined agenda; they can meet formally and define the agenda in each instance; they can meet on an as-needed basis with or without an agenda.

"Project-based learning" goes a step further. Teams of teachers are formed and work on a self-defined project or on projects assigned by the administration. Such teams can be professional learning committees. The project can involve curriculum development, space reorganization, defining new uses for technology, identifying the best way to keep drug dealers off the campus.

"Small learning communities" include both teachers and students who stay together, learn together, and develop personal relationships that could not exist if too many people were involved. They are easier to form in small schools. They can, however, also be formed in larger schools. At this instance, the school follows the lead of corporations that have broken themselves down into smaller business units in order to improve communication and interaction and make the production process more efficient. Large schools can break grade-level populations down, not necessarily through tracking students but perhaps randomly, those assigned to each segment moving through the curriculum together with the same advisors and with as many of the same instructors as possible.

Finally, we have "teacher empowerment." This has to be limited when talking about the development of curriculum owing to state and federal government regulation. In terms of delivery systems, however, it does not need to be limited. There are four levels of empowerment. The first is, "I tell you what to do and how to do it, then you do it." The second is, "I ask for your ideas, then tell you what to do and how to do it." The third is, "You decide what to do and/or how to do it, but I have the right to veto your decision." The fourth is, "You decide what to do and how to do it. I function as a facilitator and offer any assistance you might request."

We are talking about the fourth type of empowerment. Teachers take the lead in designing delivery systems and in supporting each other, perhaps through team teaching, or through professional learning committees, or through learning communities. Empowerment will be the best way to get teachers to think creatively; empowerment will be the best way to facilitate teachers reaching their full potential, especially if they have been assured of administrative support.

But this is a big "if."

18.4 Teacher Empowerment as the Biggest Challenge

How many readers have heard of a teacher or group of teachers asked to think creatively, or to come up with better ways of facilitating the learning process? How many have heard of a teacher or group of teachers who have done so, then were slapped back into line because what they proposed doesn't fit into the mold, a mold that had previously produced acceptable results, a mold that would be too difficult to change, partially because changes in any social system, including educational systems, are bound to threaten somebody with the power to block them.

By way of example, today's teachers are forced to live with a dilemma that is adversely affecting their work lives. Traditionally, their charge has been to facilitate the realization of student potential. At the same time, previously mentioned grade inflation has become a serious concern. How do we meet both challenges? The authors spoke recently to a college professor who had fallen victim to these conflicting priorities when she was being considered for tenure. We learned that she was extremely popular with students; they filled her classes; she received excellent student evaluations. We were told that students who had studied with her said she was extremely knowledgeable in her area of expertise and that she made what she taught easy to grasp, interesting and fun, that walking past her classroom during a session, one frequently heard laughter.

The professor did not receive tenure. The major problems, apparently, was that she consistently awarded above-average grades.

Why should teachers be disturbed by this story? Well, let's see. Since the professor delivered her message well, students learned more. They also studied harder, wanting to pay her back for her support. As a result, they were better prepared for her tests, did well, and got higher grades, which should have been cause for celebration. But it was not, at least in this case.

The more paranoid rationale given by rank and tenure committees for punishing teachers whose students consistently earn above-average grades is that such grades are awarded so that students at the end of the semester will give the teacher good evaluations, which, in turn, will influence the rank and tenure committee's decision. No doubt exists that sometimes this actually happens. But is the sacrifice made to guard against such cheating worth it? Also, isn't such logic an insult to our students? What is being insinuated is that they are interested only in grades and don't really care about learning—that we can teach them "butkus" and still get good evaluations if we give them high grades.

This is difficult to believe. Even if it might happen in some instances, we must again ask why students would become more interested in grades than in learning? Were they born this way? Or were they conditioned by a highly competitive education system and a highly competitive culture that encourages them to do whatever it takes?

On a more personal level, how many teachers sit down after exams, pursue their grade sheets worrying that too many of their grades are high, or low, and go back over the papers looking for places to drop or add a few points? How many teachers add something more obscure the next time they give the test, or more obvious, to make it harder or easier, in order to adjust grade levels? How many teachers, before a test, decide not to offer a review that covers key points and encourages students to truly learn what the teacher considers important? How many teachers allow students, instead, to flounder through in order to hold grades down to the desired levels?

Something is definitely out of whack with our education sector's student evaluation system and teacher evaluation system. Both are too often counter-productive, stifling innovation and creativity in the name of conformity. As a result, students suffer, teachers suffer, society suffers, and that is just the tip of the iceberg.

18.5 Measurement That Makes Sense

The United States, possibly because of our highly competitive culture, is obsessed with measurement. Although, of course, important, a key ingredient to progress, measurement, when overdone, can also become a serious barrier. In the corporate world, when "quality improvement" was the buzzword, corporations poured millions of dollars into efforts to design a means of measuring the contribution of changes in manufacturing or service systems, management systems, and the work environment to increase productivity. None of what they came up with, however, worked, because every systems change has ripple effects and incorporating all such effects into the calculation was impossible. The only accurate measure, it turned out, was the improvement in customer appreciation, in sales, in the long-term bottom line, and the most effective way to improve these things, it turned out, was to encourage all employees to identify and make improvements in their areas of expertise, to truly empower employees.

In the academic world, this translates to worrying less about finding the best way to grade students and focusing more on discovering ways to empower their instructors. A class grading system, as has been said, cannot possibly take into account all the variables that affect a student's performance and, therefore, is an inaccurate measure, limited in its usefulness. The alternative to it truly empowers teachers, whom we equate to employees in a factory or bank or office, to turn them lose to identify possible improvements in pedagogy and process administration, and then to encourage them to take the lead in making the involved changes. The bottom line, the performance of students on their comprehensive, universal exams taken at the end of secondary school, a grade the teacher has no direct influence over, should be the most accurate measure of the teachers' effectiveness.

18.6 Once Again, Standardization versus Reflective Thinking

In our discussion concerning how best to empower students and teachers, how best to evaluate them, we have once again run into the diametrically opposed foundational need for standardization and for a creativity-enhancing approach. Both are required if the education system is to serve its role. Concerning standardization, first local government, then state government, and then the national government have worked to create educational standards within their domain. Standardization is necessary for the creation of a "level playing field." It is necessary for an accurate comparison of individual student achievement. It is necessary in order to compare the progress of individual schools and of individual school districts so that weaknesses can be identified and addressed.

The problem comes when the emphasis on standardization shapes not only curriculum and approaches to the measurement of achievement, but also creates a mold into which students are force-fitted no matter what natural talents they might have. We saw an attempt to create such a mold during the Industrial Revolution Period when the Mechanistic School of Thought dominated education theory. In modern times, Japan might be the best example of a society struggling with the "mold-mentality" and the insular intolerance it eventually breeds so that new ideas are neither encouraged nor tolerated.

Concerning creativity, the classroom freedom necessary to development of individual student potential has been sought since education became a major pursuit in the western world. Creativity is the wellspring of progress. Creativity results from

a well-developed thought process that includes first compre-
hending all the puzzle pieces, then doing whatever one wants
with those pieces. The major problems with a creativity-driven
approach to education are, first, the logistical issue of allocat-
ing the necessary time, of finding enough staff, and, second, a
lack of standards by which to measure progress, by which to
make sense out of such a class. How do we ensure that students are progressing rather than just spinning their wheels?

Standardization dictates the step-by-step manner in which
a task is to be accomplished. Creativity says, "Do your own
thing." There is no way the two can be effectively combined
in any single moment. It is either one or the other so that
proponents of the two schools of thought are continuously
battling, the balance of dominance swinging back and forth
through the ages.

In modern times, the Obama administration, building on
the efforts of the George W. Bush administration, is trying
to institute national standards. At the same time, the cry is
going up for more student freedom, for students to be able
to spend more time pursuing their own interests. When
people are pursuing their own interests, they are generally
solving problems—how best to maintain my car; why birds
in flight all veer at the same time; how best to cut down on
the number of infections picked up by patients treated in
hospitals.

In the academic world, the cry for more student freedom
is encouraging a project-based curriculum that calls for reflective or critical thinking in students; that calls for students to
improve their ability to think things through in quest of the
best answer. John Dewey, considered the father of the modern day reflective thinking movement, said that students learn
the most, that they learn what is most valuable in terms of
life skills when they are solving problems. He was talking not
only about math problems but problems in all areas, prefer-
ably problems the students are already interested in addressing, or problems they develop an interest in addressing as a

result of questions posed by teachers to encourage them to think reflectively.

18.7 Why neither Charter Schools nor Vouchers nor Private Schools Provide the Answer

In the 1990s, the previously mentioned concept of charter schools was developed in an attempt to gain at least some freedom from traditional governmental bureaucracy and regulation so that staff could focus more time and energy on meeting the needs of students and would be freer to innovate. During this period, the previously mentioned voucher system was also put into place, students from poor families living in poor districts being awarded vouchers by the government so that they could attend better-run public schools in other districts, so that they could attend private schools in their quest for a better education.

   Neither of these approaches, however, according to those tracking the efforts, seemed to have made much difference in terms of student achievement. Cecelia Rouse and Lisa Barrow documented these findings in their article *U.S. Elementary and Secondary Schools: Equalizing Opportunity or Replicating the Status Quo?* According to them, "there is little empirical evidence that either charter schools or school vouchers improve student test scores. For example, three sets or researchers—using statewide data from North Carolina, Florida, and Texas, respectively—have studied whether students who attend charter schools have higher test score gains than students in traditional public schools. Their findings were remarkably similar; there are no additional achievement gains for students who attend charter schools" (Rouse and Barrow, p. 115). A study of New York City school voucher programs conducted by William Howell and Paul Peterson was also cited in this article. The authors reported that, "After three years, the study found that there were no test score gains among the students…who actually took advantage of the voucher offer and attended private schools."

What is the reason for such disappointing results? Nobody can pinpoint it. There are almost endless possibilities and combinations of possibilities. One factor, however, or one combination of factors that common sense and a vast majority of the involved research points, is the student's life outside school. Charter schools, public school, and private schools (unless students are housed on campus) all have little direct influence on this part of the student's life. They lack the resources to do so effectively; they lack the authority. Private schools, however, owing largely to the cost involved, attract students from wealthier families who do not have to hold jobs after school, who can walk through their neighborhood safely, who are not intimidated by the tremendous difference between their own background and that of fellow students.

A popular movie, *The Blind Side*, vividly portrayed this difference. The lead character—a poor, black, youth who lived in a dangerous Black ghetto—was accepted into an upper-class private school. His chances of succeeding, of not flunking out were nil until a wealthy white family took him into their home with all of its advantages.

One of the few ways to actually improve academic performance that is almost unanimously agreed upon has to do with class size. According to Rouse and Barrow, "smaller class sizes seem to be one promising avenue for improving school quality for disadvantaged students" (Rouse and Barrow, p. 116). Probably, "and for all students" should be added to the sentence.

This is an advantage attributed to private schooling. It is not necessarily that the teachers are better in private schools, but that the classes are usually smaller, which, one might think, is an argument in favor of the voucher system. Give everybody who wants one a voucher. Allow students to attend a private school with smaller-sized classes, with greater access to the individual attention missing in over-crowded public schools. But, then, with a great number of students shifting to private schools, wouldn't the same problem arise?

18.8 Tracking, More Harm Than Good?

Another part of our education system that has come under increased scrutiny and is being seriously questioned is the previously mentioned "tracking system" that was developed during the Industrial Revolution era. As has been said, it is the practice of testing students and, based on test results, assigning them to different academic tracks—honors, college prep, professional/vocational or, more recently, advanced placement (AP), general, career/technical—where the curriculum is designed to most effectively meet their needs and interests according to their measured capabilities. Once assigned, the individual students are normally stuck in the same track until they graduated from high school. In some schools, things have loosened up so that teachers can recommend a student for advanced classes in one subject area: say mathematics, when the student excels in that area but not necessarily in others.

The assumptions underlying the practice of tracking are being seriously questioned today. In Anysia Mayer's article, *Understanding How U.S. Secondary Schools Sort Students for Instructional Purposes: Are All Students Being Served Equally?*, three of these assumptions are discussed. One is that intelligence is measurable, innate, and unchanging. The second is that curriculum must be brought down to the level of the students rather than the students up to the level of the curriculum. The third is that students with different levels of potential should be sorted into groups and that different groups should be given different types of curriculum based on their intelligence and their future occupation.

The practice of tracking can have serious negative effects on the student. Young people tend to believe what they are told by respected elders or by those they understand to be figures of authority. "I have been told that I'm not smart enough to make the honors track. So be it. But because I'm not that smart (and intelligence tests don't lie), I'm not expected to do that well and, therefore, don't need to work that hard, to do my best, because even if I do my best, I'm not going to improve my situation, not going to be moved to a more prestigious track." Studies suggest that tracking even broadens the achievement gap between the different groups. Curriculum is made less challenging to help ensure that students in the college prep and vocational tracks succeed. This again decreases the amount of effort required.

It is time for tracking to go. Deciding a young person's academic future when he or she is entering adolescence leaves too much room for error. Some kids are simply slower to develop than others. By way of example, another family friend of ours, also a professor, has a son who was awkward, shy, unsure of himself through grade school and into junior high. When he took the tracking test he was told that he had qualified only for the general tract, missing the advanced placement tract cutoff by several points. Disagreeing with the decision, the father went to the school and argued until the administration realized that he wasn't going to back off and decided to move his son, along with the children of several other parents who complained, to the advanced placement track. Our friend's son now had a goal, something worth working for—to prove that he belonged in the advanced placement classes. Eventually, he graduated as a Merit Scholarship Finalist and is now studying for his PhD. But what would have happened if his father hadn't been a college professor who understood the system?

18.9 The Limitations of IQ Tests

What advocates of tracking are being faulted for is their belief that IQ is a complete measure of intellectual potential when, in actuality, it is not. It focuses only on certain parts of that potential. What it cannot take into account are equally important things such as "emotional intelligence," which has to do with the individual's ability to control and utilize emotions in order to achieve personal goals. Also, what it cannot take into account are equally important things such as creativity. Most current test of IQ focus on a very narrow definition of intelligence, on a definition of intelligence based on logical–sequential or linguistic thought processes. Unfortunately, such tests are unable to measure any form of intelligence that lies outside this predefined range.

Despite the degree of acceptance that Gardner's Theory of Multiple Intelligences (1983) has gained, modern testing continues to ignore, for the most part, spatial, kinesthetic, musical, interpersonal, naturalistic, and potentially existential intelligences. Obviously, this tendency can be attributed in part to the difficulty of designing a test capable of accurately measuring such a broad spectrum of abilities. But should academicians not be concerned by the possibility that the testing which is now increasingly foundational to our education system currently represents and reinforces the outdated values and modus operandi of that system as it now stands?

How can an education system be designed to maximize the potential of individuals if the included testing does not accurately address all facets of that potential? For example, "interpersonal intelligence," one's ability to work and get along with others, has proved to be a more accurate predictor of success in the workplace than either linguistic or logical–mathematical intelligence; yet, most schools fail to provide evaluation of this critical area.

Currently, there is a movement to get rid of tracking, to develop a common core curriculum, and not to dummy it down for anyone. With this approach, instead of earning an easy "A" in a general science course dummied down, traditional vocational track students will more likely earn a "C." But those students will be learning a lot more, especially if they receive individual attention. Also, there it is again, the "individual attention" factor that seems to be the best way, maybe the only way to improve student performance.

But, of course, opposition has arisen to the "detracking" movement. The "local elite," according to Wells and Serna, are against it. These are the same people who played a role in the earlier story about Ray, the teacher who decided that all his students should do what was necessary academically to earn "A"s. These are the parents who oppose grouping students from all levels together in classes, their belief being that such classes won't progress as rapidly, that the classes won't cover as much material, that the more capable children won't receive the desired amount of individual attention because teachers must necessarily focus on slower students (Wells and Serna, pp. 93–118).

Again, as a result of our current, outdated approach to teaching, an approach that still fails to adequately address the major challenges faced, the local elite's argument has merit, creating another win–lose situation, another situation in which one group has to be deprived when, as a result of recent advances in technology, such a trade-off is no longer necessary.

Chapter 19

The Impossible Becomes Possible

19.1 Historical Progress of the U.S. Education System

Historically, development of the U.S. education system has followed a common sense progression. During the first phase, during the colonial days and up to the 1800s, emphasis was on designing and putting into place a network of schools—primary schools, secondary schools, private four-year colleges and public universities, graduate schools, and community and junior colleges—that provided education for all, as well as a hierarchy of administrators to manage the network.

While curriculum was also a consideration during this earlier period, it became the major concern during the late 1800s and throughout the 1900s—what should be taught at each level, then what should be included in each class offering of each subject. The current movement toward universal standardization of curriculum is an end product of this phase. Also, however, is the resistance to standardization, those against it saying that standardization stifles the development of individual student potential.

Not only the United States, but the entire modern world has recently entered the third major phase, the introduction of technology to the learning process and the use of this technology, especially computers, to allow all levels of the education hierarchy to provide quality instruction in required subjects, as well as in subjects of interest to students, in ways that heighten their grasp and appreciation of the desired information. We are struggling now to design the most effective sociotechnical interface. What is the best way for students and technology to interact?

All that has happened historically is part of the education sectors' never-ending effort to increase the amount of useful learning students do in the classroom and to improve the teacher's ability to provide such learning. As Corcoran and Silander say in *"Instruction in High Schools: The Evidence and the Challenge:"*

> For student outcomes to be more equal or, perhaps more reasonable, for substantially all students to master the core knowledge and skills needed for further education, for success in the modern economy, and for responsible civic participation, educators will have to vary the amount and nature of instruction to take account of students' differences in motivation, dispositions and aptitudes, experience, and instructional needs. At the moment, however, as the review of evidence in this articles demonstrates, neither researchers nor educators have an adequate idea of how to do that (Corcoran and Silander, p. 174).

19.2 Still Seeking the Best Approach

As we still don't have the answers, teachers continue to work toward them using a technique called "adaptive instruction."

The teachers are learning as they go, trying something new (or old) and then developing a tool or technique for assessing the outcome. If the results are good, they try it again, perhaps with minor modifications that might improve the outcome. If the results are not good, teachers restructure the approach or try something else.

One of the most serious challenges to those involved in adaptive instruction is, once again, the design of an effective way to measure the progress resulting from the involved modification. But how does one isolate the effect of the modification from that of the myriad of other previously mentioned factors affecting a student's daily academic progress? This is a question perhaps impossible to answer. Also, ideally, we would need to find the right adaptation for each student, which, quite simply, is impossible when a class of any size is involved. Teachers would, ideally, have to draw up a lesson plan for individual students and modify the plan continually to meet the student's evolving needs.

So, the discussion returns to our quest for ways to provide more individual attention to students when the numbers involved make such a scenario highly difficult to achieve, if not impossible. It's not that teachers are not trying, but everything we come up with falls short, even combinations of things that we come up with fall short.

The core problem concerning this challenge might actually be that we are starting from where we are, from where we have been traditionally, trying to move forward from there. We are, as the saying goes, still thinking "in the box," trying to patch the current model, shifting periodically from the need for more standardization to a quest for more freedom, then back to the need for more standardization, then back to the quest for more freedom, without really moving forward, without altering our paradigm in ways that would give us a better chance of meeting current cultural needs; in ways that would give us a better chance of taking advantage of current possibilities.

As has been said in Chapter 1, we are not fully taking into account the powerful potential of the modern day technology now at our disposal, technology that, if utilized properly, could make possible an "and" situation rather than the traditional "either/or" situation in terms of the standardization versus creativity argument; that would allow teachers to deliver the basics to all, but, at the same time, provide the attention to individual students that seems to have become the "holy grail" of twenty-first century education; that would help teachers become more effective.

19.3 Updating the Attitude of Teachers

One of the things we have to focus on before introducing a new approach to education that makes more effective use of computer technology is defining the changes necessary in the way classes are run, for, as we know, the most useful technology is of no use unless those in charge are willing to take advantage of it. In the education sector, concerning those who are in charge, we find the same situation that we find in the current business sector. This should come as no surprise. Both sectors are a product of the same growth ethic culture and are moving toward the same development ethic culture. In education, we find two types of teachers—those who can be equated to workplace "bosses" and those who can be equated to workplace "facilitators."

Boss-type educators want strict control over all activities. They define what is to be learned and do most of the teaching. Grades are seen mainly as a necessary lever, as a way to get students to accomplish what is required. Boss-type teachers expect students to listen carefully and quietly, to take good notes, to read all the assignments, to remember as much as they can, and to regurgitate what is required for tests. Their approach is dull but forceful. It varies little from class to class. There are few surprises.

The newer breed of facilitator-type teachers has more fun. These people want students to get involved and to think as much as possible. They want students to reflect. They want students to interact and to learn from each other. They want students to practice working in teams so that they might be prepared for future employment. But, at the same time, facilitator-type teachers still feel the need to maintain control. Classes are too large for them to function otherwise. They still set the curriculum and have the final say on individual and team activities. They want students to be creative, but within predefined parameters. They still decide who is doing well and who is not. They still run the show, though student input is welcome and encouraged.

The teacher's traditional responsibilities include

1. Dissemination of information.
2. Teaching students how to generate their own information.
3. Teaching the rules, tools, and techniques necessary for the effective use of information.
4. Making sure students receive all the educational pieces required to function productively in society.
5. Making sure students understand each piece and its uses.
6. Helping students figure out useful ways to combine these pieces.
7. Ranking students so that they can be "fit" into the right growth-ethic workplace slot.
8. Cultivating individual potential.

Cultivating individual potential normally lies way down on the priority list. This, again, is not because teachers, at least facilitator-type teachers, don't think it is important. Rather, it is because of the previously mentioned class size and time constraints and because of the fact that information, rules, tools, and techniques are the building blocks and, therefore, must come first.

Again, there is a progression here. Originally, schools were one room, one teacher affairs with all ages combined. The purpose was to give individual students the most basic of skills necessary to functioning in society—reading, writing, and arithmetic. Eventually, as the curriculum expanded and class size remained relatively small, as more levels of education became available—secondary school, college—increasing opportunity arose for students to focus on and develop their individual potential.

But then, as the new nation was born, became better organized and increasingly industrialized, a deluge of immigrants arrived and class size grew. Emphasis switched from the individual to the group. The teacher's role now was to ensure that all class members achieved a certain level of education. Efforts to cultivate individual potential were no longer possible. In most quarters, they were no longer desirable. The mold mentality took over. People talked about an army of workers emerging from our education system in lock step to become part of a "well-oiled machine."

Dissent, of course, arose. But the industrialist's philosophy held sway until the late 1800s and early 1900s when developmental psychology became popular and emphasis shifted gradually back toward the individual, so that currently, an uneasy balance exists between the two, between the still strong "mechanistic" and the "human relations" schools of thought.

19.4 The Current Challenge

What we are trying to figure out at this point in the progression is whether this is an either/or situation that will remain so forever, or whether there is a way to combine the strengths of the two approaches and create a new approach that lifts every student to that level where they can contribute meaningfully to the economy and to society while, at the same time, developing their individual potential fully. We are trying to discover a model that makes this possible when our classes are large and impersonal. We are trying to discover a way to get our teachers out from between "a rock and a hard place."

An interesting thing happened while the authors were trying to think this challenge through. During the summer, we took a break and canoed down the Mackenzie River in the Northwest Territory of Canada. Real wilderness, small communities of the indigenous population, of "First Nation" Dene Indians, appeared occasionally among the trees along the shoreline. Stopping at one of these communities, we were fortunate enough to meet the local schoolmaster who taught all grades in a two-room schoolhouse. Obviously, our first question was, "How do you teach second, sixth, and tenth graders all at the same time?" As a response, the schoolmaster showed us the computer lab where students work by themselves when not in class with her.

Obviously, our second question was, "Are students limited by the computer assignment programs in how far they can progress?" Her response to this was, "No, students can progress as far and as fast as they want, so long as they pass the required computer-administered tests along the way. In fact, one of our eleventh graders is already working on college sophomore-level math problems. For him, all I do is make myself available when he has questions."

So, there it lay, the answer to our quandary, the answer to the education sector's modern-day dilemma, an answer made possible by combining the original colonial approach to education with modern technology.

19.5 Putting the Pieces in Place

One of the most exciting bodies of research we have reviewed covers the work being done at the Institute for the Learning Sciences at Northwestern University founded in 1989 by Roger

Schank. The work is exciting in its own right, but when one views what is said in the context of the development ethic, the implications become downright startling.

Schank's emphasis is on two things. Conceptually, it is on providing students with the information necessary "to do something they already want to do" rather than forcing them into traditional patterns of learning. Technically, it is on developing computer programs that make learning even the basics more interesting, challenging, and fun.

In terms of the latter, electronic situations are being created. For instance, assume a student, through a computer program, enters a store to buy something she wants. The cashier actually appears on the terminal screen to ask her questions, to tell her that if she buys 10 widgets instead of just one, they are all half price, to ask how much that would be if one widget costs seventeen cents?

A value of this approach, of course, is that it uses familiar, real-life situations. Another value is that if the student makes a mistake, it is brought to her attention immediately and dealt with while still fresh in her mind, rather than the student being forced to wait until the homework is corrected the next day, or until the test is passed back. A third value is that the student can "stop the teacher" and go back over a situation as many time as desired, with elaboration, if desired, and not worry about holding up the rest of the class.

Also, when the student makes a mistake, it is not made in front of other student with possible negative connotations. In fact, making mistakes becomes a positive learning experience because the program immediately helps the student work them through with no one else involved, with no embarrassment. This scenario helps students shift their emphasis from getting it right the first time in order to win applause to being willing to take risks because they know that, right or wrong, they'll gain from their effort.

From the developmental perspective, however, the major advantage of sharing traditional teacher responsibilities with computers is the conceptual one. Quite simply, the advantage is that such an approach allows each student to gain the individual attention we have been talking about for centuries. Computers can provide at least a large part of that attention. They can also help free the teacher from traditional responsibilities so that the teacher can provide more of it.

Computers are generally better than humans at disseminating the required information and introducing the requisite tools, techniques, and rules. They can be excellent at helping individual students understand information, tools, techniques, and rules. They can be excellent at teaching students how to integrate pieces and how to use them effectively. Computers are also capable of showing students how far they have progressed, which is more important than ranking them when one talks developmentally.

19.6 Self-Management as the Key to Learning

Perhaps the greatest difference made possible by the effective incorporation of computer technology into education, however, is that students will have the support necessary to progress at their own rate. This difference, in itself, destroys the traditional educational paradigm, at least at the lower grade levels. Minimum achievement requirements will be set in individual subjects and in terms of overall academic progress. But there will be no limits at the other end of the spectrum, at the maximum end. There will be no age-based ceilings in terms of what can be offered, as there are now for most children. If something is interesting or challenging or fun to a student, that child will be able to just keep going, at home as well as at school, during vacations as well as in the school year, with parents or friends assisting as well as teachers.

Also, the computerized system will allow us to integrate subjects more easily. The basics all can be combined in a single problem-solving scenario where students not only must understand the relevant information, the range of tools and techniques available and how they fit together, but also must establish priorities, deal with ethical issues, address new problems that suddenly appear, and so on. In the workplace, employees are beginning to gain more control over their jobs. In the realm of education, with these innovations, students will begin to gain more control over what and how they learn.

The best example we can offer concerning the benefits of this arrangement involves another family friend. As part of their desire to produce well-rounded, well-developed children, our friend Jason and his wife, like a great number of other parents, encouraged their two sons to take up musical instruments. Their oldest son, Dane, eventually settled on the piano. In his second year of lessons, while he was still plodding through the second level, Dane and Jason went to a movie. The ten-year-old boy apparently heard a song, part of the musical score, that he really liked. On the way home the son asked, "I want to learn to play that song. Can you get the music for me?"

My friend told me that his first inclination was to tell the boy that he wasn't ready for such a challenge, that he should stick with his lessons, concentrate on the basics, and not try to jump ahead, that he should wait for a couple of years so that he wouldn't end up frustrated. But, instead, my friend swallowed his parental, father-knows-best, boss-type response and replied, "Sure."

Jason bought the sheet music and gave it to his son. The following Saturday morning an unusual thing happened; the father awoke to the sound of piano notes. It was unusual because Dane had never before practiced without being told to do so. About half an hour later, Jason wandered into the den where his son was still trying to figure out the piece's opening.

Dane said, "This is tough."

The father listened for a while, then asked, "What part of the piece do you like the best?"

Dane responded, "The middle part."

"Then why don't you start there?" Jason suggested. "You can always come back to the beginning." His son thought that a good suggestion and soon had his first line learned.

About a month later, Jason found Dane struggling again with the beginning of the piece. The boy was trying to play both hands but couldn't fit them together properly. Jason listened for a while, then suggested, "Why don't you learn one hand first, then the other, before trying to put them together?"

"I've already done that," his son replied.

"All right, then," Jason said. "What if I play one hand and you concentrate on fitting the other into it?" His son liked this second suggestion, so they worked together for a while.

Approximately four months after he started Dane could play the piece through. His instructor said that during this same period, he had made a quantum leap in terms of his overall learning and had shown musical potential the teacher had never before suspected.

What had happened? Quite simply, the child had found something he was interested in, had been allowed to pursue it in his own way, at his own rate, with his father and his piano instructor functioning as facilitators. Their role had been to answer questions and to make suggestions that the student could accept if he wanted to. At the same time, however, the boy was still learning the basics from his music teacher, which made more sense to him now that they helped him move toward his private objective; toward something he was personally interested in accomplishing.

Individuals accomplish the most when they've defined their own objectives and have gained control over the pursuit. Individuals learn the most when they are given access to the necessary inputs and then are allowed or encouraged to teach themselves. And the ability to teach themselves is developed when students are given the opportunity to practice self-management. These things have been known for centuries. But it is only now that we have access to the paradigm and the technology necessary to provide such an opportunity for everyone.

Computers have already been used in an increasing number of instances to help teachers provide the basics. But now they can also help us giving students the opportunity to take control and build on these basics as they wish, to progress at their own rate, and to receive the requisite individual attention, first from the computer itself and, when that does not suffice, from the teacher.

19.7 Our Traditional Grading System Made Obsolete

Since computers allow us to progress at our own rate in each subject, and as the progress of individual students in different subjects will obviously vary greatly, our growth ethic grading system will become obsolete. The growth ethic system, the main purpose of which seems to be to compare, is based on an upper limit concerning what is to be learned by members of a class. Those who reach that limit or come closest to it receive "A"s. The grades of the rest depend on how well they do in terms of the "A" requirements, or on how well they do in terms of the "A" students.

But in the new world development ethic model, with the help of computer technology, not one but two tiers of student evaluation will be made possible. The first tier will relate to the required curriculum, to students learning the basic tools of education. Students' progress will be judged by the level at which they are working in terms of what is expected at that age. Individuals can be above the age expectation or below it. The second tier will include the level of progress achieved by individual students in the computer-driven self-education portion of their education.

As has been said, there will be no upper limits for students in these latter realms. There will also be no outer limits. In the computer-driven realm, they can focus their efforts in one subject matter area or divide their attentions among several. They can pursue advanced studies in, say, history alone, or in mathematics as well as history.

In terms of a traditional grading system by which individual progress or the absence thereof is measured and compared to that of others in the class, our new system will encourage students to compete more so against themselves than against peers. Emphasis will be more so on cultivating personal strengths, on improving personal performance in weak areas, on achieving personal goals, than on beating classmates.

Chapter 20

Dealing with the Logistics of the New Paradigm

20.1 Meeting the Initial Challenge

With this new paradigm in place, the school day—at least during grade school, junior high school and high school—will be divided into three different types of activity. Each student will have access to a computer terminal or terminals. Part of every day, usually the morning session, will be dedicated to learning traditional academic subjects—mathematics, English, history, the sciences, languages, geography, and so on. The subjects will be addressed one at a time, the curriculum having been set for all schools by the National Department of Education.

Students in each grade will be required to reach a defined level of proficiency in each traditional subject. Some will reach it quickly and will be encouraged to continue on some would have reached it during the previous school year or during the summer break and will continue from where they left off. Some will have trouble reaching it and will need help, the help being provided mainly by teachers who are now functioning mainly as facilitators, or by more advanced student functioning as tutors.

Such tutors can be used at the primary school level as well as at the junior high school and high school levels. In this instance, the tutor will also benefit. It has long been realized that one of the best ways to learn something is to teach it. Also, those willing to work as tutors can be paid. When several students basically at the same level are having trouble meeting a challenge in a subject, the teacher or tutor can take them away from their class or computers, bring them together in a small focus group, and work to improve their understanding before they return to the challenges presented by the teacher or computer program.

While at the primary school level, students will remain in the same room for the entire day for all subjects, those in secondary school will move between rooms, from the English teacher's room to the history teacher's room, to the mathematics teacher's room. It would be possible to rotate the instructors instead, with the students remaining in the same room while the instructors move. This latter arrangement would save time. But the instructors couldn't bring along supporting materials—wall maps, charts, diagrams, models, and reference books—that are of value. Also, students wouldn't get the chance to roam around some, to clear their minds, and to talk to friends.

The second part of the school day, the "practical-experience" part, will involve hands-on activities with a focus on students learning how to work together and interact in a team atmosphere. Students will work on projects defined by a teacher, breaking down into project groups. No formal level testing will be required. Grades will be pass–fail. Computer programs can be developed to support the practical-experience sessions as well, but hands-on, team based activities will play the central role.

During the third part of the day, the self-education part, students can pick an academic subject or several subjects, a technical skill or several technical skills, or a combination thereof and teach themselves. Teachers will continue in their facilitation role, as will student tutors. In this instance, students in junior high school and high school will move to the chosen subject-defined classroom or workshop on a first-come-first-serve basis. If there is overflow in a computer-driven self-education subject, part of another classroom and its computer terminals can be commandeered. If there is an overflow in the workshop self-education realm, say too many students want to study automobile maintenance or pottery, some will have to find another skill to work on until the operation can be expanded.

20.2 Encouraging and Measuring Progress

The standards for level achievement concerning traditional academic subjects will be set nationally by the Department of Education. Students who do not pass the level exam for a required subject can retake the exam after studying more. The questions in the repeat exam, though calling for the same degree of understanding, will obviously be changed. If a student cannot pass the required level exam after several attempts, it will be left to the teacher's discretion as to whether or not that student should be allowed to advance at the end of the school year. Such a decision would be required when, for example, the student was doing extremely well in all subjects except math. If allowed to advance to the next grade, however, the student would continue to study at the lower level in math, trying to catch up.

The teacher can also decide not to allow a student in this situation to advance to the next grade. The chances of a teacher not allowing the student to advance would increase as the number of required subject areas that the student falls behind in grows, as the number of required subject area level exams the student is unable to complete successfully increases.

Previously, it has been pointed out that modern communications technology is much better at delivering information to students than teachers. It can provide a far greater and more comprehensive range of information. It can make the information more interesting. The computer programs used in this approach will be developed by private companies working on government contracts. Emphasis during their development will be on creativity. The programs will be designed to entertain as well as to teach because people learn more when they are enjoying themselves. Sesame Street, which both entertains and teaches could obviously be a good model, at least initially, for the design of lower grade programs.

This approach to education will also create a more cooperative atmosphere. Earlier in the book we talked about how the pursuit of knowledge differs from the pursuit of money, both being necessary resources. As there is always a limit to the amount of money available, people compete for it. But there is no limit to the amount of knowledge available. We are always, so to speak, "printing more" and the more we print the better off we are. Our traditional grading system is based on a monetary philosophy of distribution. The number of good grades available is limited, so students have to compete for them. But since there is no limit to the amount of knowledge that can be generated, everybody should benefit each time a student reaches a higher level of understanding.

With this understanding in place, students will be more prone to work together. Cooperation will replace competition as the driving force in the classroom or wherever they are studying. As has been said, students will be able to work on the required subjects as well as on the individualized portion of their learning at home as well as at school. Teachers and tutors can suggest what they should focus on during nonschool hours, but cannot require it. Tutors can be paid to make themselves available via e-mail or cell-phone to answer questions from students or from groups of students working together during nonschool hours.

In terms of meeting college or university requirements, grades, as we know them, will obviously no longer be available to admissions departments. Rather, all level exam scores will be recorded; whether students have passed or not, their resume of achievements continuing to grow. This will be done for required subjects as well as for academic self-education studies. These scores will be made available during the admission process as well as the teacher's comments on the student's progress and attitude.

Also, at the end of secondary school, students will be tested in each required subject area. Following several days or weeks of study, a series of exams similar to the SATs and ACT tests but more comprehensive, more similar to those given in European countries, will be administered. Although students might have completed several advanced levels in a subject, say chemistry, they will still be required to take the comprehensive exam at the end of secondary school that covers the basics. Colleges and universities will be given access to the results of these tests as well.

20.3 Breaking Down Traditional Boundaries

Having the freedom to progress at one's own rate will also help break down the traditional boundaries between age groups, between grade school, high school, college, and graduate school. A high school student might be at the college sophomore-level in language or sociology and at the tenth-grade level in history or biology. A college freshman might already be doing graduate work in physics.

Is it possible, then, that the traditional school as we now know it, with age-group segregation, will disappear? I don't think so. There is a third side to the education coin in the new world. This side complements both the standardized basic subjects learning and the realization of individual potential sides and is also necessary to achievement of the development ethic on a societal level. This side has to do with learning how to interact and to work effectively with others, which means that the age-based classroom situation, or some variation in it, will remain necessary.

Students who want to function effectively in the new world society and workplace, no matter how well developed they are individually, must learn how to pool their talents and expertise in order to produce richer, more acceptable, more easily implemented results. Research has provided strong evidence that, in most instances, groups do better at solving problems, at making improvements than do individuals. But for the group approach to produce good results, participants must learn how to interact effectively, and the best way to learn how to interact is by doing so with appropriate guidance.

Education in group-interaction should begin at the lowest levels of school and should progress especially in parallel with the practical-experience portion of the day. The pass–fail evaluation, in this instance, should be based on the individual's interaction with his or her group. This approach might be difficult at first and produce complaints ("I did most of the work!" "It was my idea!"). But it will help prepare students for what must become their workplace reality, a reality where emphasis is more so on combining resources to make projects successful than on distributing individual credit.

The next question is, "How can we successfully orchestrate the practical experience emphasis-on-interaction-and-teamwork segment of the education process?" This is where the teacher comes in. The teacher would monitor the individual progress of students and will build practical-experience teams around projects that interest participants. The teacher or an advanced student tutor will facilitate project team meetings. These people will help to keep the effort moving and function as a resource. At the same time, they will be teaching group process skills, but "on-the-job," so to speak, rather than in the traditional classroom, from-the-book setting.

There will also be activities that allow the class as a whole to interact—field trips followed by class discussions; project team presentations followed by class discussions. As a result, with this model there will be two types of interaction that teach students how to work together, how to relate effectively—project group interaction and the class-as-a-whole interaction.

Again, grades, as we now know them, will no longer be relevant. While the group as a whole will be evaluated on the project's success, comments will be made on each individual member's ability to participate which, in this instance, is more important than what the individual student contributes. The facilitators will evaluate the strengths and weaknesses of individual team members and work on group process skills.

20.4 Including University-Level Work in the Loop

Concerning university and graduate school-level education, academicians should stop reinforcing the old top-down approach in the classroom and begin empowering their student in the way that business managers are beginning to empower employees in the workplace. Professors should encourage a more participative atmosphere and begin sharing their procedural decision-making responsibilities and power with students. Emphasis at this level, more so than at the primary or secondary school level, should be on a team approach. Again, two types of activity will take place. During the first computers and professors will provide the basics. Individual students will be encouraged to advance their studies in required subjects as well as in subjects the student desires to pursue. The involved work, of course, can go on during class or during the student's free time.

During the second activity, the team approach will be stressed. For example, at the beginning of the semester, the professor will present an outline of topics to be covered along with a basic text and a list of supportive readings, then announce that, from that point on, students will teach that part of the class. Teams will be formed around the topics. Their responsibility will be to research the topic, to prepare a presentation, to deliver the presentation, and then to lead a discussion.

Similar to self-directed work groups in the business world, the teams will be responsible to the professor for the final product, but will control their activities in generating that product. They will generate their own presentation materials, maybe bringing in actual problems and examples from the real world. The professor, during this part of the class, will function again as a facilitator—encouraging the teams, helping to identify sources of requested additional information, checking on team progress to make sure members stay on track, fleshing out presentations when necessary, reviewing and stressing key points, helping coordinate the efforts of different teams to avoid overlap, and taking the lead in tying the presentations together into a meaningful whole. This role is obviously similar to the role manager's play today in progressive companies that have adopted the team approach to production.

Teams can put on plays, sponsor-friendly competitions between nonpresenting teams, or demonstrate new approaches. Students in the audience will receive a brief outline of the main points covered in the presentation. They will also fill out a brief evaluation following each presentation, listing both its strengths and things the team needs to work on. The professor, after reading the evaluations, will consolidate them and pass them on to the presenting team along with his or her own comments and will grade the team effort. Presentation grades will be pass–fail. They will be based mainly on content but also partially on style, on creativity, and the ability to stimulate class participation. This approach will discourage verbatim readings from the text and other resources while encouraging team members to support each other's efforts. If a team fails a presentation, it will be required to give another one on a different subject before the end of the semester.

Advantages of the team-based presentation segment of the course include

1. Students learn the advantages of a team effort and how to work effectively as a team member.
2. Research skills are enhanced.
3. Rather than trying to beat each other, students concentrate on learning from each other and effectively integrating their knowledge.
4. The required attitude helps shape participative workplace habits.
5. No matter how well prepared the instructor might be, group efforts and group discussions generate more information than lectures.
6. Presentations help make courses more interesting.
7. Students get a chance to practice presenting themselves and controlling sessions.
8. The professor frequently learns something new and is at less risk of suffering burnout.

20.5 Time to Move on toward New World Education

In summation, the opportunity now exists for education systems to help individuals realize their full intellectual potential while, at the same time, making sure that all students reach the level at which they can function successfully in society and make a contribution. The opportunity now exists to standardize educational requirements while, at the same time, encouraging creativity in terms of how these standards are achieved and in terms of how far beyond them students can progress.

The technology we need to bridge the involved gaps and to realize these traditional objectives has finally arrived.

At this point, therefore, the major obstacle to the desired changes is no longer "out there," and it is no longer a lack of appropriate pedagogy or technology. Rather, the major obstacle resides in ourselves, in the way we think, in the difficulty we have accepting new ideas no matter how beneficial they might be. Once we can get beyond this obstacle, however, we can turn the corner and be on our way. We can leave the growth ethic behind and move toward a development-ethic-based education system that, in turn, will move us toward a development-ethic-based society.

The involved challenges can now be dealt with, as soon as we decide to do so.

Bibliography

Ackoff, R. and Emery, F., *On Purposeful Systems*, Piscataway, NJ: Aldine Atherton, 2005.

Aldeman, C., *What US Higher Education Can Learn from a Decade of European Reconstruction*, Washington, DC: Institute for Higher Education Policy, 2008.

Bowers, C.A., *The Progressive Educator and the Depression: The Radical Years*, New York: Random House, 1969, p. 24.

Brookes, M. and Huisman, J., The Eagle and the Circle of Gold Stars: Does the Bologna Process Affect US Higher Education? *Higher Education in Europe*, 34(1), 2009.

Brown, F.L. *Educational Sociology*, New York: Prentice-Hall Inc., 1947.

Bryson, B., *At Home: A Short History of Private Life*, New York: Doubleday, 2010.

Button, W. and Provenzo, E., *History and Education and Culture in America*, 2nd edition, Boston, MA: Allyn and Bacon, 1989.

Cave, P. *Primary School in Japan: Self, Individuality, and Learning in Elementary Education*, New York: Routledge, 2007.

Charlier, J.-E. and Croche, S., The Bologna process: The outcome of competition between Europe and the United States and a stimulus to this competition, *European Education*, 39(4), 2007–2008.

Convey, A. and Kerr, K., Exploring the European dimension in education, *European Education*, 37(4), 2005–2006.

Corcoran, T. and Silander, M., Instruction in high schools: The evidence and the challenge, *The Future of Children*, 19(1), 2009.

Cremin, L., *American Education: The Colonial Experience: 1607–1783*, New York: Harper and Row, 1970.

Cremin, L., *American Education: The National Experience, 1783–1876*, New York: Harper and Row, 1980.

Cubberley, E., *State School Administration*, Boston, MA: Houghton Mifflin Co., 1927.

Cubberley, E. (ed.), *Readings in Public Education in the US: A Collection of Sources and Readings to Illustrate the History of Education Practices and Progress in the US*, Cambridge, MA: Riverside Press, 1934.

Daun, H., Globalization, EU-ification, and the new mode of educational governance in Europe, *European Education*, 43(1), 2011.

Doi, T., *The Anatomy of Dependence*. Trans. John Bester, Tokyo: Kodansha International, 1973.

Doi, T., *The Anatomy of Self*. Trans. Mark A. Harbison, Tokyo: Kodansha International, 1985.

Dower, J.W., *Embracing Defeat: Japan in the Wake of World War II*, New York: W.W. Norton & Company, 1999.

Enache, R., Building national unity and curriculum uniqueness in the European context, *Petroleum–Gas University of Ploiesti Bulletin*, 62(2), 2010.

Feldman, D. and Benjamin, A., Creativity and education: An American retrospective, *Cambridge Journal of Education*, 36(3), 2006.

Froebel, F., *Pedagogies of the Kindergarten*, New York: D. Appleton & Company, 1895.

Gates, B., Shame is not the solution, *The New York Times* Op-Ed Section, A23, 2012.

Griscom, J., *A Year in Europe, Knight*, Reports.

Grissmer, D. and Flanagan, A., Exploring rapid achievement gains in North Carolina and Texas, *National Education Goals Panel*, 6–7, 1998.

Hanushek, E. and Raymond, M., Does school accountability lead to improved student performance? *J Pol'y Analysis and Management*, 21, 2005.

Hofman, R.H., Hofman, W.H.A., and Gray, J.M., Comparing key dimensions of schooling: Toward a typology of European school systems, *Comparative Education*, 44(1), 2008.

Howe, D.W., Classical education in America, *Wilson Quarterly*, 2011.

Ishii, Y., *Developmental Education in Japan*, New York: Routledge Falmer, 2003.

Josephson, M., *The Robber Barons*, New York: Harcourt, Brace and Company, 1934.

Kerr, A., *Dogs and Demons: The Fall of Modern Japan*, London: Penguin Books, 2001.

Krug, E., *The Shaping of the American High School*, vol. 1, New York: Harper and Row, 1964.

Ladson-Billings, G., From achievement gap to education debt: Understanding achievement in US schools, *Education Research*, 35(7), 2006.

Lesser, G., *Children and Television: Lessons from Sesame Street*, New York: Vintage Press, 1975.

Mayer, A., Understanding how US secondary schools sort students for instructional purposes: Are all students being served equally? *American Secondary Education*, 36(2), 2008.

Meny, Y., Higher education in Europe: National systems, European programmes, global issues, can they be reconciled? *European Political Science*, 7, 2008.

Metzger, W., *Academic Freedom in the Age of the University*, New York: Columbia University Press, 1955.

Molesworth, R., *An Account of Denmark as it was in the Year 1692*, Copenhagen: Rosenkilde and Bager, 1976.

Noble, S., *A History of American Education*, New York: Rinehart and Company Inc., 1954.

Okano, K. and Motonori, T., *Education in Contemporary Japan: Inequality and Diversity*, Cambridge: Cambridge University Press, 1999.

Raubinger, R. and Piper, W., *The Development of Secondary Education*, New York: Macmillan, 1969.

Reber, S., *School Desegregation and Educational Attainment for Blacks* 2 (National Bureau of Economic Research, working Paper No. 13193, 2007)

Roth, I., *Japanese Identity Dependency in Society: How it Affects the Education System*, Unpublished.

Roth, I., *Using Learning Technologies to Teach Multiculturalism in Japanese Primary Schools*, Unpublished.

Roth, W., Keeping the jungle out of MBA classrooms, *Personnel*, 1990.

Roth, W., Computers can individualize learning and raise group-interaction skills, *The Education Digest*, 65(3), 1999.

Roth, W., *The Roots and Future of Management Theory: A Systems Perspective*, Boca Raton, FL: St Lucie Press, 2000a.

Roth, W., Helping academia realize its potential, *Technos*, 9(2), 2000b.

Roth, W., *Ethics in the Workplace: A Systems Perspective*, Upper Saddle River, NJ: Pearson Prentice-Hall, 2005.

Roth, W., Yes, tests still rule: Shifting our emphasis back to learning means more, not less, standardization, *American School Board Journal*, 2005.

Rouse, C. and Barrow, L., US elementary and secondary schools: Equalizing opportunity or replicating the status quo? *Future of Children*, 16(2), 2006.

Rousseau, J.J., *Emile, or on Education*, New York: Dutton Press, 1911.

Sass, S., *The Pragmatic Imagination: A History of the Wharton School*, Philadelphia, PA: The University of Pennsylvania Press, 1982.

Schilcht, R., Stadelmann-Steffen, I., and Freitag, M., Educational inequality in the EU, *European Union Politics*, 11(1), 2010.

Schoppa, L.J., *Education Reform in Japan*, New York: Routledge Press, 1991.

Seybolt, R. *Source Studies in American Colonial Education, The Private School*, Bureau of Education Research, University of Illinois, Vol. XXIII, No. 4, Bulletin No. 28, 1925.

Smith, P. *Japan: A Reinterpretation*, New York: Vintage Books, 1997.

Spring, J., *American School, 1642–1996*, 4th edition, New York: McGraw-Hill, 1994.

Sudhir, K., *Frederick Taylor: A Study in Personality and Innovation*, Cambridge, MA: The MIT Press, 1970.

Tomusk, V., Three Bolognas and a pizza pie: Notes on institutionalization of the European higher education system, *International Studies in Sociology of Education*, 14(1), 1004.

UNESCO, *World Education Report 1995*, Paris, 2005.

US Department of Education, *The Improvement of America's Schools Act of 1994, Reauthorization of the Elementary and Secondary Education Act (1995)*, available at http://eric.ed.gov/ERICWebPort

USA Today, Principals Too Quick to Use "Teacher Shortage" as an Excuse, August 27, 2011.

USA Today, Love It Or Hate It, The SAT Still Rules, August, 27, 2011.

Van de Grift, W., Quality of teaching in four European countries: A review of the literature and application of an assessment instrument, *Educational Research*, 49(2), 2007.

Weiner, T., *Legacy of Ashes: A History of the CIA*, New York: Random House, Inc., 2007.

Wells, A. and Serna, I., The politics of culture: Understanding local political resistance to detracking in racially mixed schools, *Harvard Education Review*, 66(1), 2007.

Wyse, D. and Torrance, H., The development and consequences of national curriculum assessment for primary education in England, *Educational Research*, 51(2), 2009.

Zielenziger, M. *Shutting Out the Sun: How Japan Created its Own Lost Generation*, New York: Vintage Books, 2006.

Index